Ray Eames

In 1930s New York

Ray Eames

in 1930s New York

By Sarah Reeder

Ray Eames in 1930s New York

Published by Sarah Reeder

ISBN: 979-8-9855423-0-1

Reeder, Sarah

RAY EAMES IN 1930S NEW YORK

SARAH REEDER

www.artifactualhistory.com

For Ray, with gratitude for her gift of imagination

Table of Contents

Introduction

My longstanding fascination with Ray Eames has enriched my life for many years. In the late 1990s I was fortunate to have the opportunity to view the exhibition "The Work of Charles and Ray Eames: A Legacy of Invention" at the Library of Congress and I left completely intrigued with Ray Eames. I later had the chance to pursue that curiosity through several summers of research spent at the Library of Congress reading through Ray's manuscript collection, which she donated to the Library following her death in 1988.

My research focused on the years before Ray Kaiser met and married Charles Eames and founded the Eames Office together with him. Charles Eames, an extremely talented and charismatic figure in his own right, has captivated architects, designers, and art historians since he became a public figure in the mid-20th century, while Ray and her contributions have remained less well known (I once had an art history professor refer to them as "the brothers Eames" without realizing they were married). This scholarly discrepancy motivated me to focus on the years before Ray met Charles so I could isolate Ray as an individual and better concentrate on the experiences and artistic training she received during her twenties while living in New York City and studying with the painter Hans Hofmann.

In my daily life I run an art and antique appraisal firm. Every appraisal report has what is called a "Scope of Work" detailing the purpose, intended users, and outline of an appraisal assignment, and I've found it to be a useful tool to incorporate here to describe what this book is and isn't intended to be. This isn't a critique of Charles Eames, or an argument against his many important contributions to the Eames Office. This isn't a discussion of Ray Eames in the Eames Office, as the research I will be featuring here primarily focuses on her life until 1940 prior to her cofounding the Eames Office. I have found it instructive in my many years of studying artists to have a thorough knowledge of their foundational experiences and early interests. It is my hope that this volume will help create a more comprehensive understanding of Ray Eames and the training and talents she brought to the work of the Eames Office.

Chapter 1: Ray's Early Years

In 1932 a young woman wrote in a letter to her mother: "—Ah Yes—do me a favor and go to see the exhibition of Kandinsky at the Valentine Galleries. He is an abstract painter—You may have read the article on him in the Sunday times—Anyway the point of abstraction is that things are beautiful whether they happen to be chairs—apples or people—they say his color is marvelous."[1]

These were the words of twenty-year-old Ray Kaiser. When she co-founded the Eames Office she drew on a sophisticated knowledge of art and culture and a decade of formal artistic training. She spent the 1930s in New York City studying with the German painter Hans Hofmann and working as an abstract artist. In addition to her classes with Hofmann, Ray attended hundreds of cultural events and actively pursued interests in subjects such as photography and modern dance. She was a meticulous record keeper and donated her papers to the Library of Congress. Many elements of her life in 1930s New York are documented in this manuscript collection. Ray's youthful experiences in this inspiring environment influenced her work throughout her life.

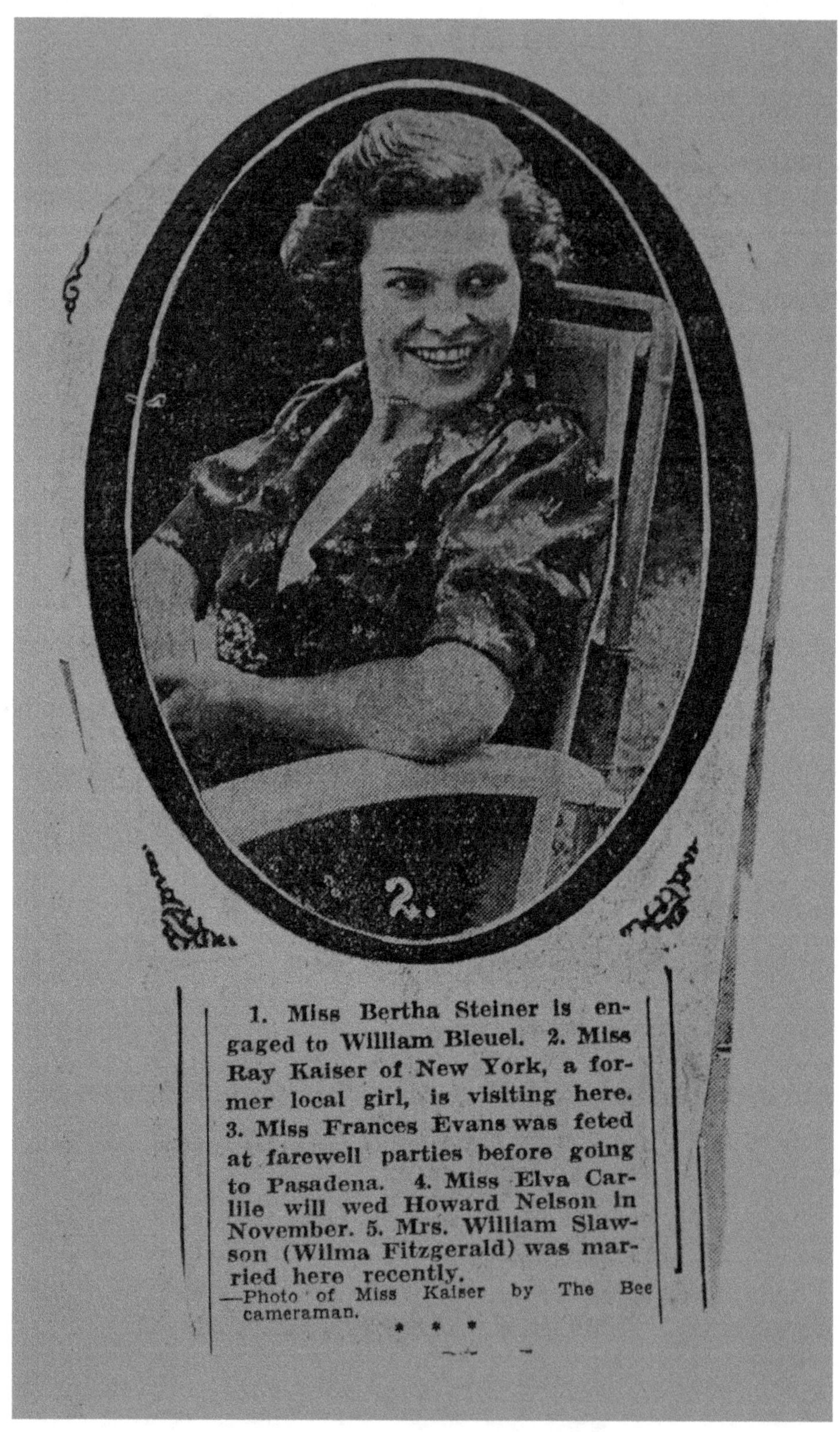

1. Miss Bertha Steiner is engaged to William Bleuel. 2. Miss Ray Kaiser of New York, a former local girl, is visiting here. 3. Miss Frances Evans was feted at farewell parties before going to Pasadena. 4. Miss Elva Carlile will wed Howard Nelson in November. 5. Mrs. William Slawson (Wilma Fitzgerald) was married here recently.
—Photo of Miss Kaiser by The Bee cameraman.

* * *

Ray Eames in the 1930s, photo taken during a visit to California and published in the *Sacramento Bee*

The Collection of Charles and Ray Eames at the Library of Congress consists of photographic slides, drawings, films and hundreds of boxes of files. Boxes 276 through 293 in the collection are the items studied most closely in this book: the Kaiser Family papers, ranging in time from 1885 to 1940. They contain "correspondence, notes, school papers, juvenilia, financial records, clippings, and art, theater, film, dance, and music programs relating to Ray Eames prior to her marriage to Charles Eames and to her immediate family."[2]

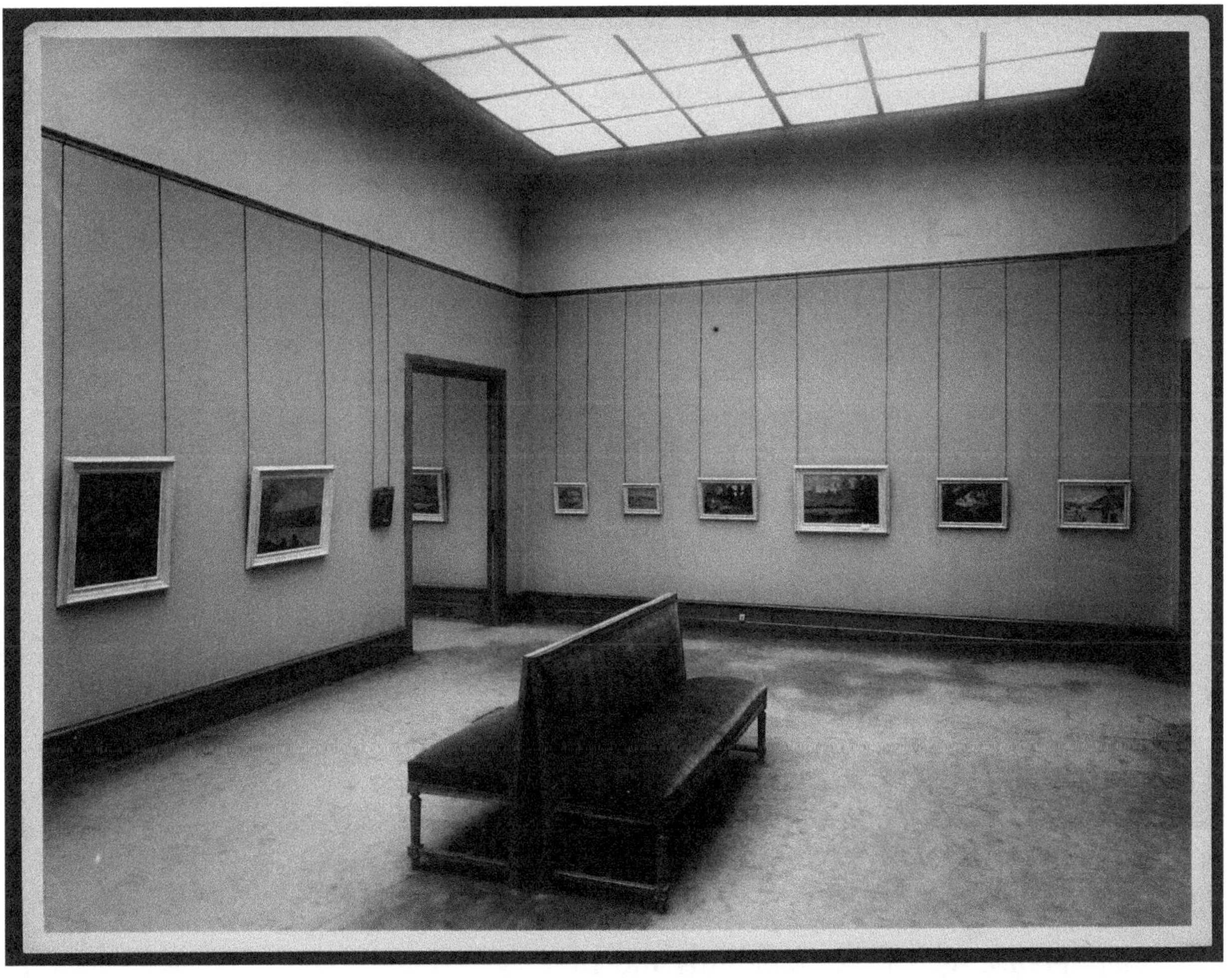

Circa 1932 exhibit installation of work of Louis Eilshemius by an unidentified photographer, Valentine Gallery Records at the Archives of American Art, Smithsonian Institution

Family and Early Life

Ray Kaiser was born in Sacramento, California on December 15, 1912. Her birth name was Bernice Alexandra Kaiser, but for most of her life she went by Ray, a version of her family's pet name.[3] Many of the early family documents refer to her as Ray-Ray. In the 1920 federal census Ray is listed as "Alexandra" rather than her true first name Bernice but by the 1930 census and in her high school yearbook she was identified as Ray. Ray's name has long been a source of confusion and speculation among scholars about her motives for why she went by a name often given to men, but there is evidence to suggest that "Ray" was part of an older naming tradition within the Kaiser family. Ray had an aunt (her father's little sister) who died several months before Ray's birth in 1912. Her aunt was named Rachel Kaiser but she was known by the name "Ray" and identified in several official federal census listings, newspaper articles, and her grave marker as Ray Kaiser.[4] In addition to his sister, Ray's father also had a cousin named Raphiel who went by Ray for most of his life, indicating "Ray" may have been a significant Kaiser family name.

The family endured another tragedy shortly after Ray's birth when her older sister Henrietta Elizabeth died in the summer of 1913. The *San Francisco Call* published the following on July 13, 1913: "In this city, July 11, 1913, Henriette Elizabeth, beloved daughter of Alex and Edna Kaiser, a native of Sacramento, aged 1 year 8 months and 18 days."[5]

Despite these losses, Ray's father Alexander Kaiser was a dynamic, prominent figure in his community who came from a line of highly creative individuals. His parents Morris L. and Henrietta Kaiser were both born in Prussia (modern-day Germany) and came to America in the mid-19th century. Morris Kaiser was a successful merchant who owned the California store Friedberger & Kaiser together with his brother-in-law Arnold Friedberger.[6] Friedberger and his wife Lotta Kaiser's children included a son named Raphiel Kaiser who also went by Ray in adulthood.

Newspaper clippings in the Kaiser family papers detail the successes of Ray's father Alexander through his evolving career as a jewelry store owner, operator of a vaudeville theater and record-breaking insurance salesman.[7] Theatre, fashion, jewelry design, and entrepreneurship were interests associated with many of Ray's relatives in her paternal line. In an online exhibit about the Friedberger family in California at the Jewish Museum of the American West, curator Samantha Silver notes that: "In 1882, Arnold Friedberger *[married to Ray's great aunt]* and his family moved to Stockton. In 1889, Friedberger sold his stores in Sheep Ranch and San Andreas. He opened a new, larger store at Sacramento and Elm Streets in Lodi with his brother-in-law, M.L. Kaiser *[Ray's grandfather]*. They named their store Friedberger & Kaiser General Store. The store remained at this location until 1935. Arnold Friedberger spoke English and German, which was helpful for talking with the German farmers who had moved to the area from North Dakota. Friedberger also worked as a Wells Fargo agent in Sheep Ranch, San Andreas and Lodi, even riding shotgun on the stage. He invested in several mining operations with other businessmen, including the father of William Randolph Hearst....

Lotta Kaiser Friedberger *[Ray's great aunt]* helped found the Women's Benevolent Society in Stockton, California. Alexander Friedberger and George

Kaiser (M. L.'s son) *[Ray's uncle]* took over the management of the family's general store in 1901. In 1935, Alexander relocated the store to 6 N. School Street. His daughter, Irma, helped turn the general merchandise store into a *women's clothing store*. Leo Friedberger ran a general store in Clements. Maurice and *Ray* Friedberger owned a *jewelry store* in Stockton. Joe Friedberger owned a *stationery store* in Lodi."[8] [Emphasis has been added to highlight the family interests in the design and retailing of jewelry, women's fashions, stationary, and other goods].

While Alexander Kaiser was of Jewish heritage, Ray's mother Edna Burr Kaiser was Episcopalian. Edna Burr was born in California in 1887 and grew up in a large family. Her father Henry A. Burr was born in Iowa and her mother Mary Evans Burr was born in California. In the 1900 federal census thirteen-year-old Edna was living with her parents and eight of her siblings in Stockton, California. Her father's listed occupation was an attorney, and his own father Lester Lorin Burr (husband of Elizabeth Evans born in Kentucky) had been a farmer born in Ohio. Edna's mother Mary Evans Burr was from a primarily agricultural lineage with members of previous generations living in Missouri and Kentucky. The 1902 City Directory for Stockton, California lists Henry A. Burr (Ray's grandfather) as an attorney along with a Miss Jessie Burr (Ray's aunt) who was is identified as a dressmaker living at the same address as Henry A. Burr. Jessie Burr was six years older than her little sister Edna, who was Ray's mother. Ray had relatives on both sides of her family involved in the fashion field.

In a 1980 interview with Ruth Bowman for the Smithsonian Archives of American Art, Ray commented,

> I feel so badly about no one knowing my parents, who gave me so much, through their interest -- they were just always interested in everything, and really seemed to be without prejudice, which I think is such a great thing to have given one.... My father's parents came from Germany, my father was born in this country, and my mother's parents, or her grandparents, I guess, came West on a covered wagon. I realize I didn't ask questions, I didn't know, and then they were gone and I had no one to ask. But they were here. They -- her family -- Burr Evans and they were here early on -- Mayflower time, and her father must have been an extraordinary man. He had been a teacher and decided to become a farmer and learn about the land. He was evidently very bad at it, but they lived in the country and had many children. I knew about country living from her.[9]

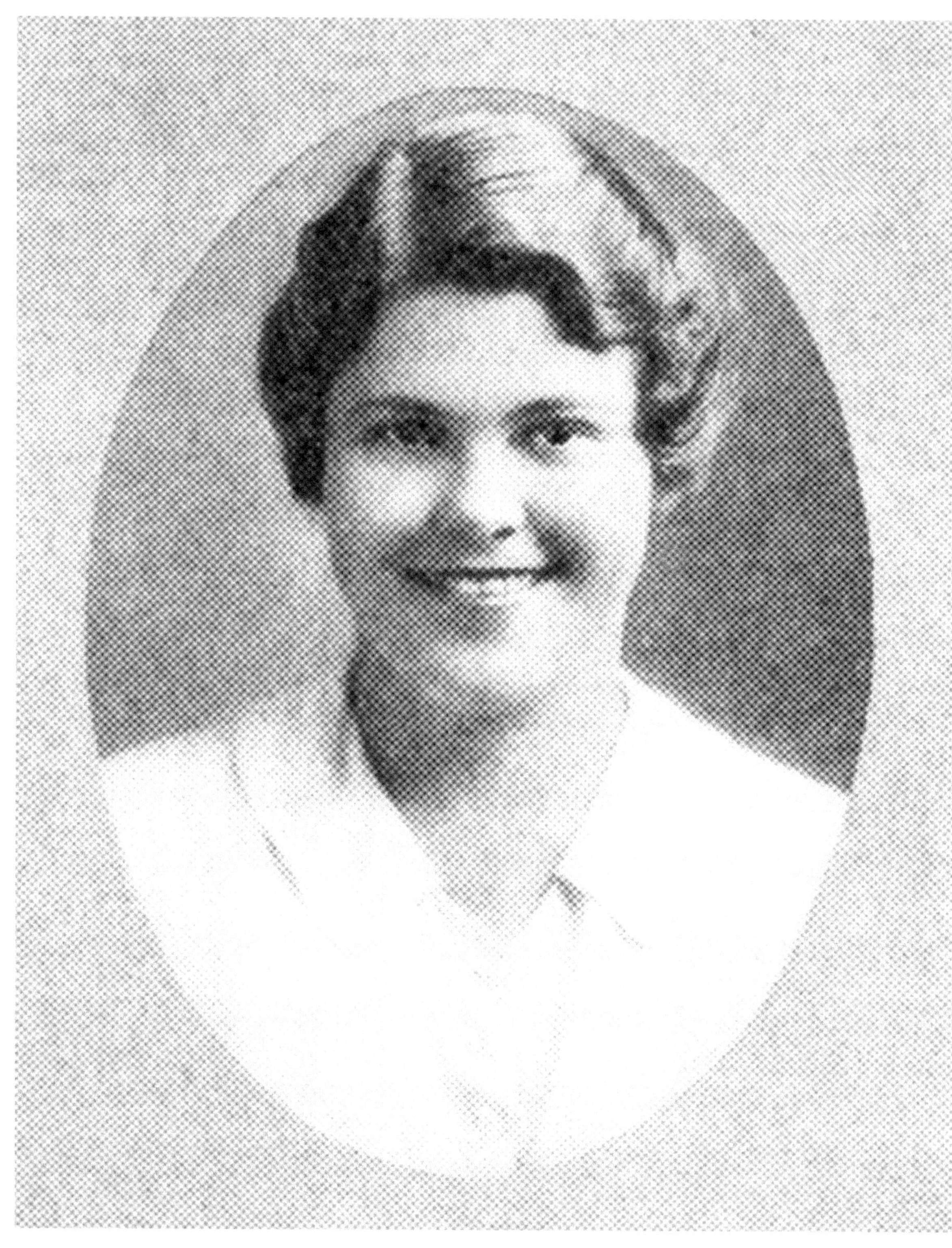

Ray Kaiser Eames in her high school yearbook picture at Sacramento High School, Sacramento, California, Private Collection

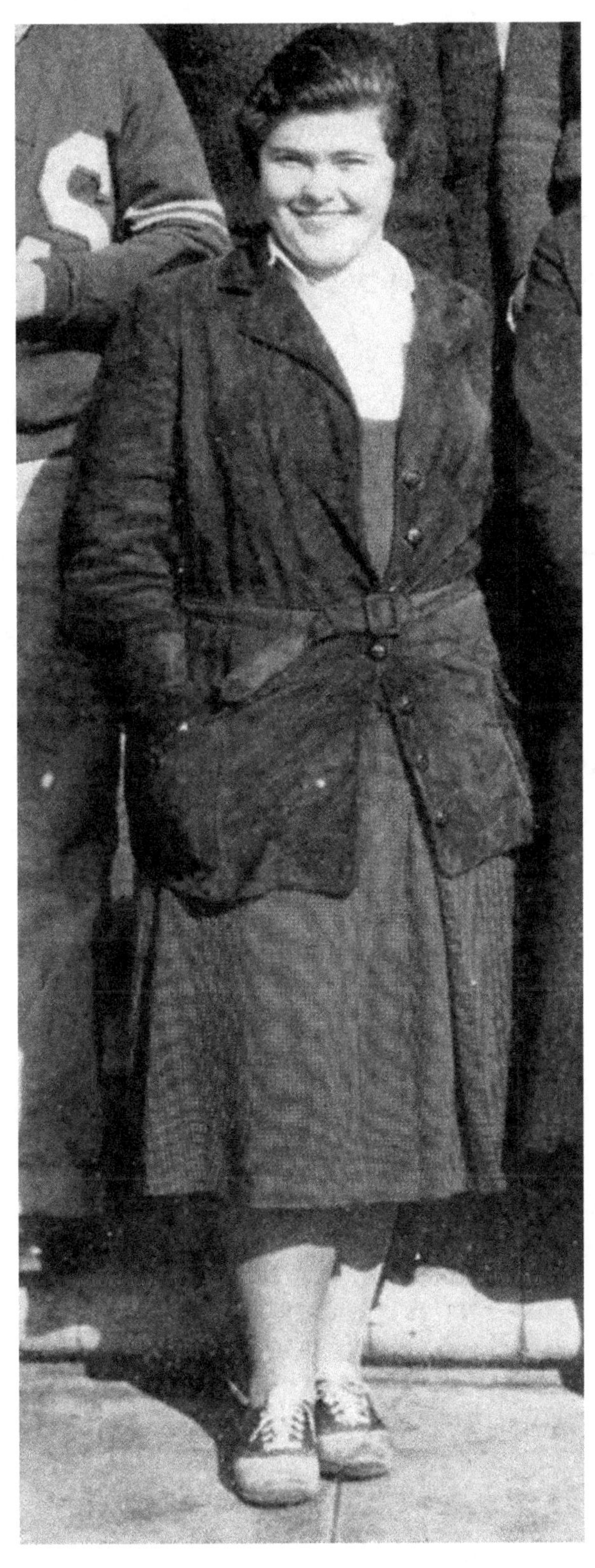

Ray Kaiser Eames in her high school yearbook picture at Sacramento High School, Sacramento, California, Private Collection

Ray's artistic inclinations began at an early age. In addition to the numerous childhood drawings contained in the Kaiser Family Papers in the Library of Congress collection, her high school yearbook lists her membership in Art Club and French Club as well as her role as a Big Sister.[10] When Alexander Kaiser died in 1929, Ray was finishing high school and her older brother Maurice was attending West Point. After a semester in a local California college, Ray and her mother joined her brother in moving to New York. Ray attended the May Friend Bennett School in Millbrook, New York for three years, following a program of art history, drawing, sculpture, dance, English and French. Upon graduation she joined her mother in New York City.

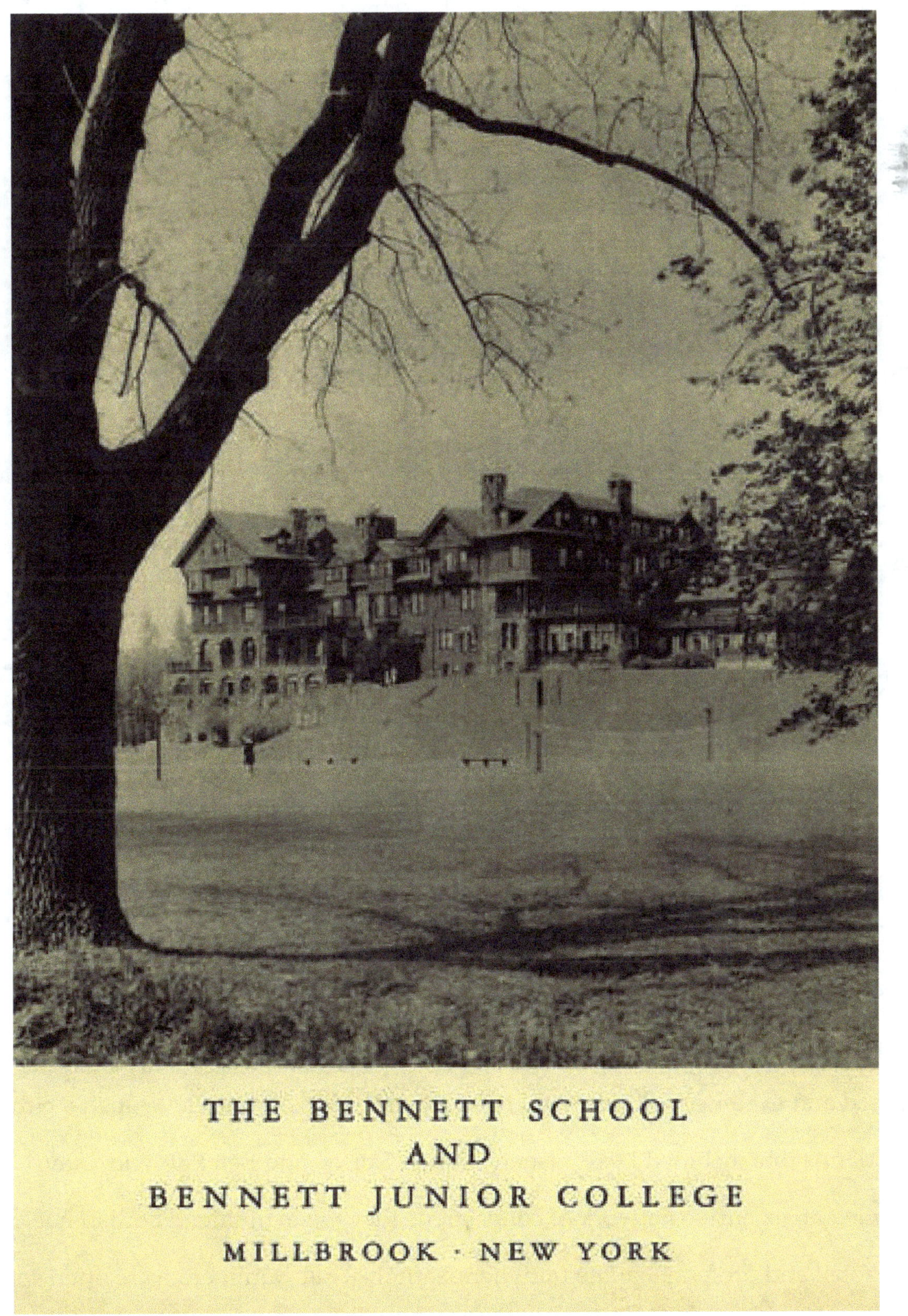

The Bennett School, Millbrook, New York, Millbrook Library, Bennett College Archives

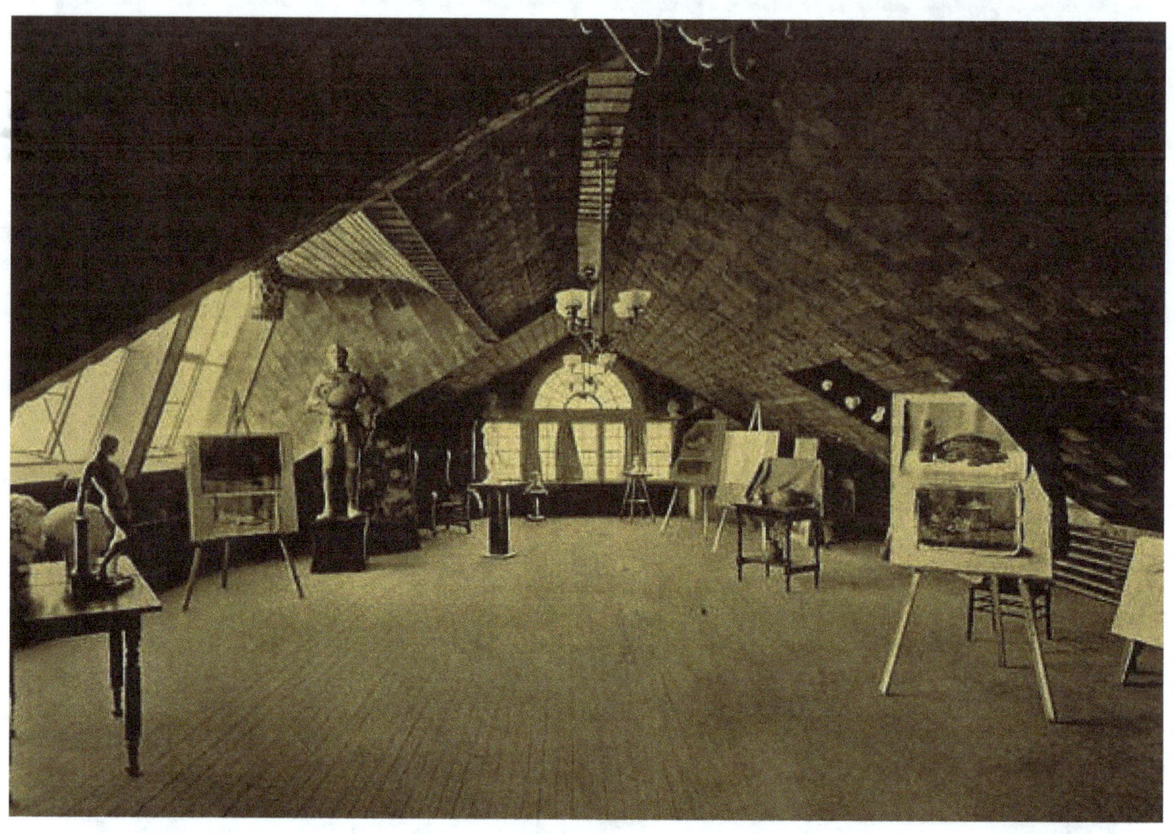

The Art Studio at the Bennett School, circa 1908, Millbrook Library, Bennett College Archives

Although her mother lived in the Barbizon Hotel, Ray found her own apartment to live and paint in. They exchanged frequent letters that form an approximate diary of Ray's daily activities. She studied with Hans Hofmann, joined and exhibited with the American Abstract Artists, and developed a circle of friends that included Lee Krasner, Arshile Gorky, and Ben Baldwin. Ray formed an extensive network of connections that she maintained both in her personal and professional life until her death in 1988. Summers were often spent in Hofmann's New England art camps.

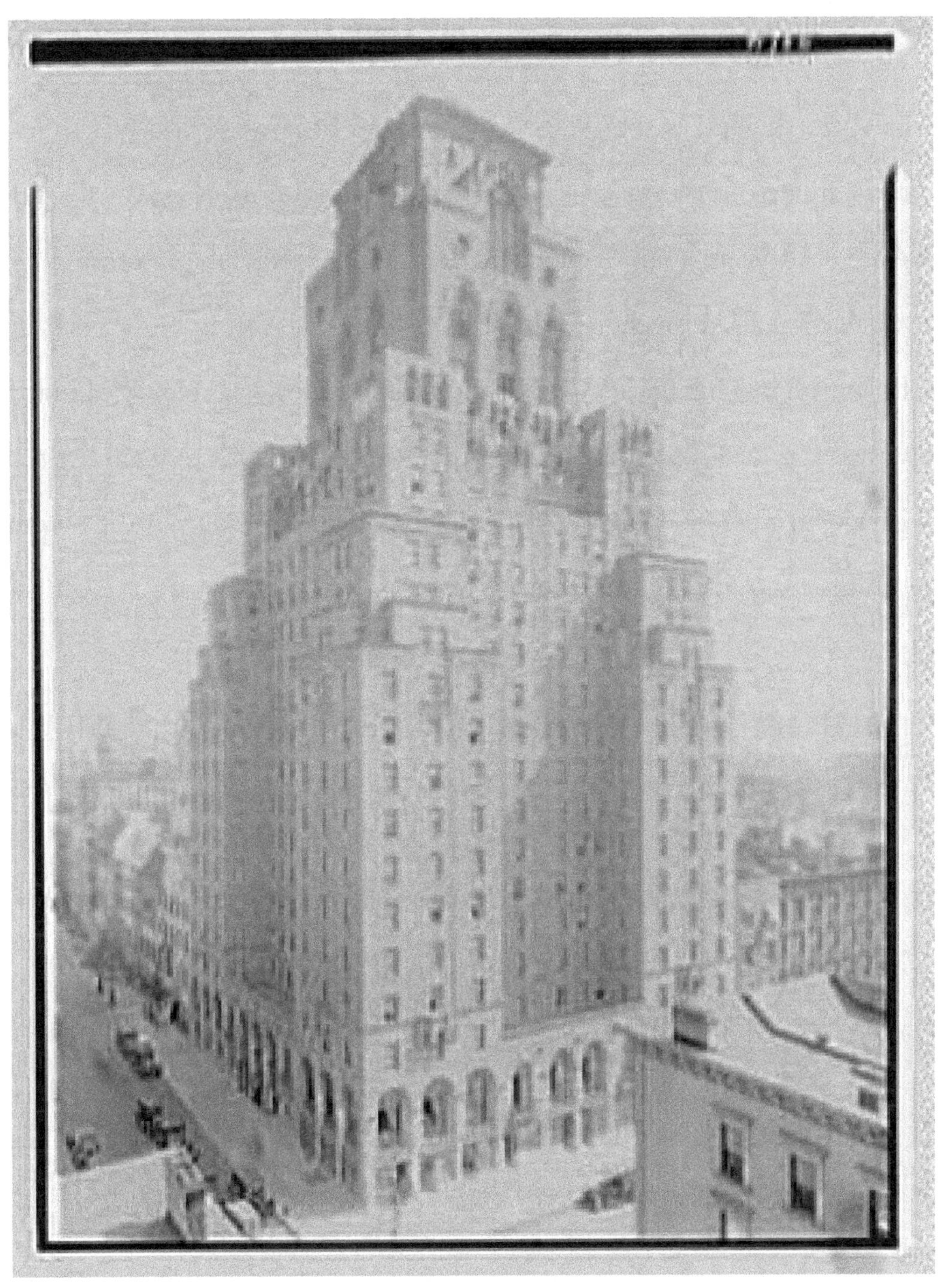

The Barbizon Hotel, Samuel H. Gottscho, photograph, 1928. Gottscho-Schleisner Collection (Library of Congress)

The Cranbrook Academy

Towards the end of the 1930s Ray's mother became ill and had to move to the gentler climate of Florida. Her sickness continued until Ray was forced to leave New York to nurse her. When she died in 1940, Ray's only remaining family was her married brother Maurice. With few ties left in New York, she decided to enroll in Michigan's Cranbrook Academy of Art. Her goal was to learn engineering and structure so that she could move back to California and build a house for herself. Characteristic of her broad interests, she also wanted to study with the renowned potter Maija Grotell.[11] While at Cranbrook she met Charles Eames.

Chapter 2: Hans Hofmann's School

Early in 1933, Ray expressed her frustration with her Bennett School art classes. In a letter to her mother dated January 16, she writes,

> I'm glad you opened Bernadette's letter—what did you think of it? I'm so happy about that girl—I can't believe she's progressed as she has. Don't you think she's wonderfully improved? I didn't realize how little I have been doing until I had her letter-I just haven't enough time to do anything—I'm going to work at one thing when I get out—At Easter Vacation let's go to the League-(Art Students League) and see how it looks. I've got to get under somebody good and learn-I'm not actually learning anything here in drawing or painting. The only thing I get out of it is the actual experience of doing it and I haven't time for that –The still life I started yesterday is very ordinary but I wanted something simple just to practice on—I'm so terribly out of practice you know—It's square—A shiny black bowl with a band of orange around the bottom and a gray enamel coffee pot with a round white plaque that looks like a dish in the background—lavender [...] wall in the back and a faded peach drape.[12]

Soon after she wrote that letter she did "get under somebody good and learn." The process by which Ray found out about Hans Hofmann is documented explicitly in letters written to her mother at the time the events occurred. Ray met Hofmann while she was still in the Bennett School. On May 15, 1933, she wrote her mother, "Guess what!—Mercy Carles is visiting here—

she came up last night late and I've seen her here and there today—But haven't had time to talk with her—Hofman [sic] the artist (the teacher at the League) drove her up and is staying until tomorrow."[13] Mercy Carles was Ray's friend from the Bennett School and a Hofmann student. Cynthia Goodman, author of *Hans Hofmann*, describes the connections between the Hofmann and Carles families:

> According to Mercedes Carles Matter, Hofmann began painting in earnest again at her encouragement during the summer of 1934, when she was one of his students at the school of his former Munich student Earnest Thurn, in Gloucester, Massachusetts. That summer Hofmann shared a house with Mercedes and her father, the painter Arthur B. Carles, whom he had first met in Paris about 1904. When Mercedes had begun studying with Hofmann at the Art Students League in 1932 she reunited the two men.[14]

Carles later married the photographer Herbert Matter, who worked in the Eames Office from 1942 to 1946.[15]

In a second letter written that night Ray stated,

"... Mercy came up to the room and told me all about what she has been learning from Hoffman [sic].... She also told me that Hoffman may be at Gloucester this summer and if so—it will be his last appearance in this country and a wonderful opportunity—From what she's said-and what I've read in an article of his I would love to study just those few weeks if I possibly could."[16]

After her graduation from the Bennett School, Ray attended the Gloucester summer art school and in the autumn went to New York City to take Hofmann's classes at the Art Students League. She continued to study with him until the late 1930s, when she had to leave New York to join her ailing mother in Florida. Hofmann and Ray remained friendly until his death in 1966. Ray displayed Hofmann paintings in the Eames House in California, and Hofmann proudly posed for a 1951 *Time Magazine* photo in front of two Eames chairs, which the photo credit proclaims were given to him by Ray Eames.[17] Hofmann's teachings profoundly influenced her aesthetic perception of the world and instilled in her a sense of structure that permeates all her work. In choosing the Eames chairs for the photo shoot, Hofmann was showcasing a product of his teaching.

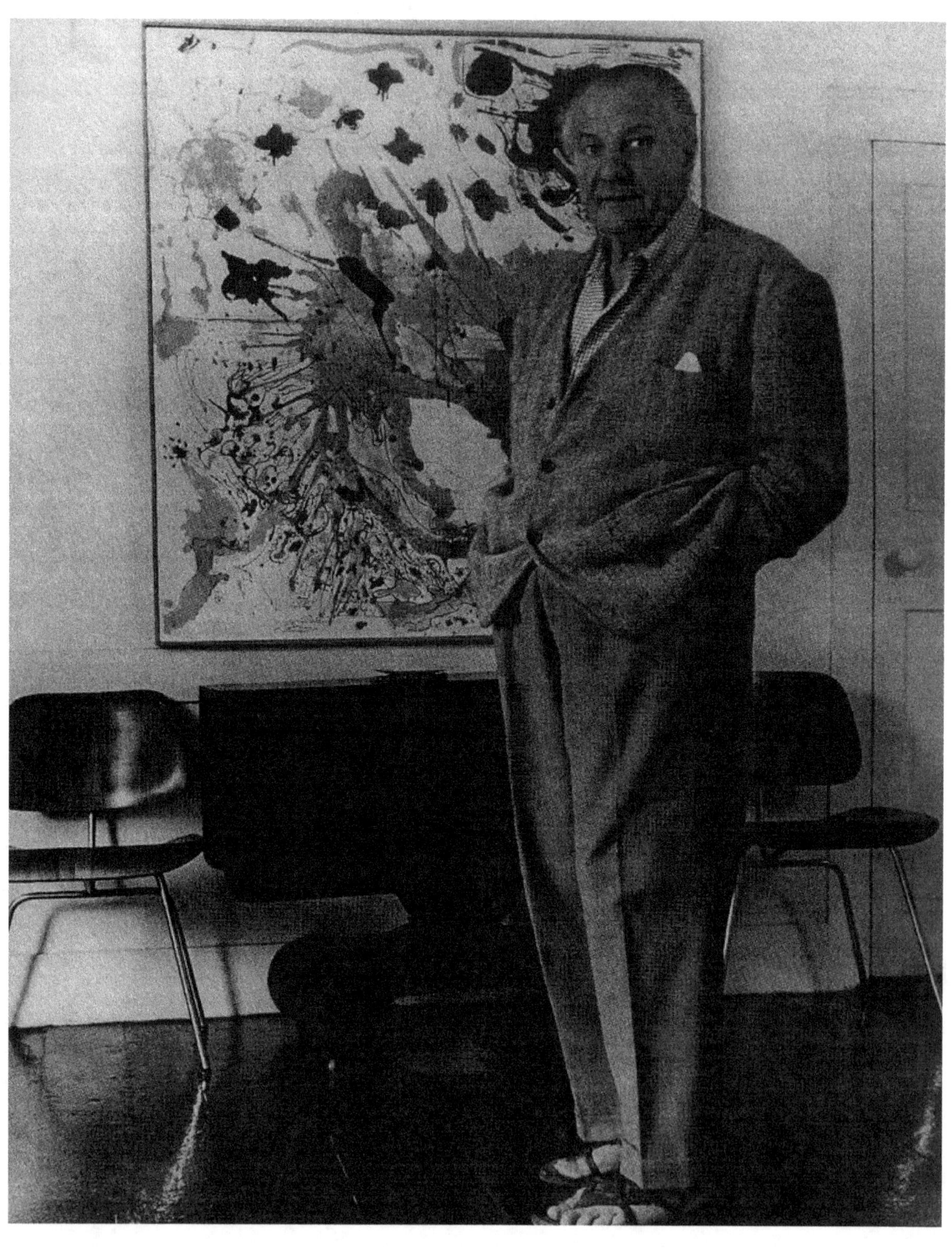

Hans Hofmann standing in front of Eames Chairs for *Time Magazine,* 1951, photograph of vintage clipping taken by the author

Hofmann's Background

Hans Hofmann was born in Germany in 1880, placing him in the same generation of fellow European artists Picasso and Matisse. An adolescent inventor and science prodigy, Hofmann spent money his father gave him for future endeavors to pay for art school.[18] This investment launched his career as a painter. A 1933 advertisement for the Gloucester summer session that Ray attended identifies Hofmann's early teachers as "the Bulgarian Court Painter, Michailow; the Munich Painter, Aspe; the Hungarians, Ferenczi and Grimwald."[19]

Until the age of fifty, Hofmann lived in Europe, absorbing the stimuli of the art world. From 1903 to 1914 he lived in Paris through the patronage of Berlin collector Phillip Freudenberg.[20] At the outbreak of World War I Hofmann was "kept out of the army by aftereffects of a lung condition" that Karen Wilkin, author of _Hans Hofmann: A Retrospective_ identifies as tuberculosis.[21] Although he was safe from the military, the war ended Freudenberg's patronage and Hofmann needed a means to support himself. In 1915 he opened the Hans Hofmann School of Fine Arts in Munich. The school was closed in 1932 due to the political climate in Germany and Hofmann settled in the United States.

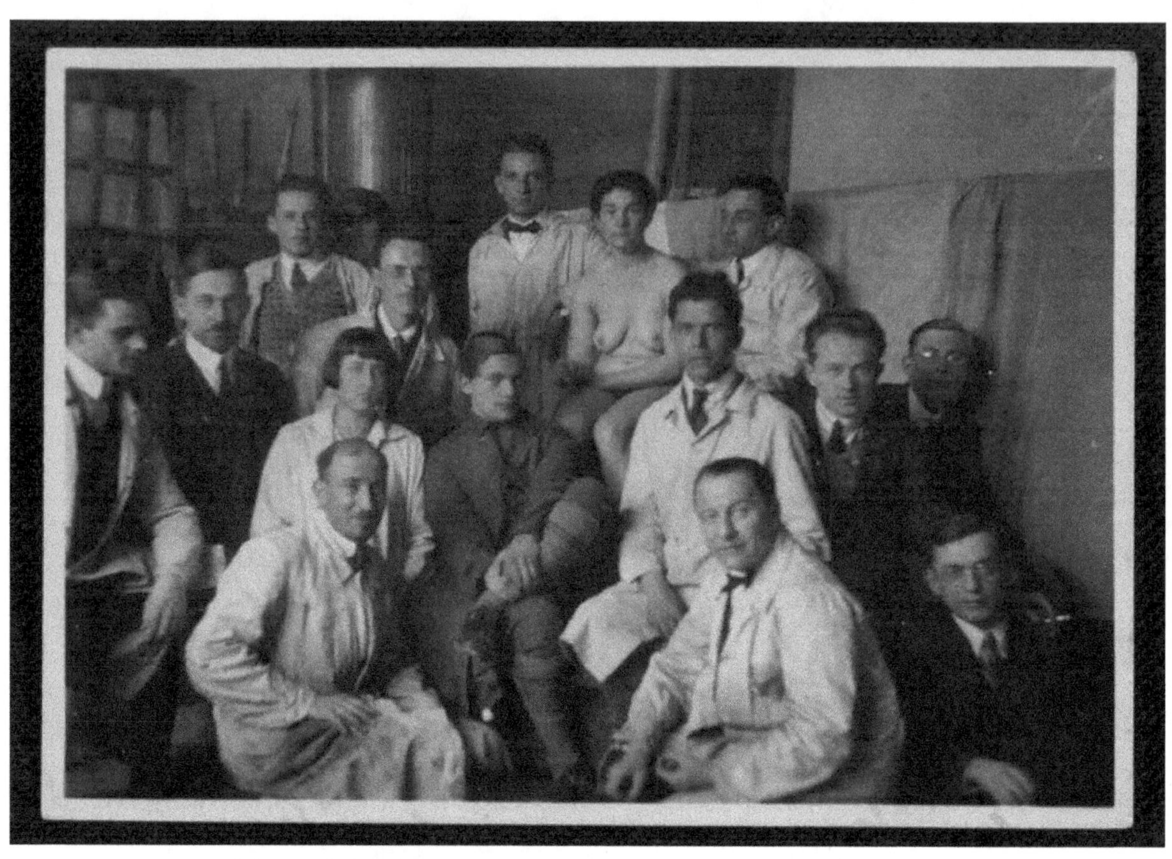

Hans Hofmann School of Fine Arts in Munich, circa 1926. Hofmann is pictured in the front row and is the right figure in the light coat and necktie, Smithsonian Archives of American Art

Hofmann in America

Wilkin states Hofmann first came to America in 1930 "at the invitation of former student Worth Ryder" to teach a summer session at UC Berkeley.[22] He went back to Munich that winter but returned to California in the spring to teach at the Chouinard School of Art in Los Angeles, and at University of California at Berkeley in the summer. In 1932 Hofmann settled in New York when "former student Vaclav Vytlacil help[ed] arrange a teaching position at the Art Students League."[23] Goodman writes he lived in the Barbizon-Plaza Hotel, which explains the hotel stationary of the New Year's Card he sent to Ray which remains among her papers.[24] Addressed to the endearingly spelled "Budha," his nickname for her, the inside of the card contains a number of pencil sketches.

Wilkin writes in 1933, Hofmann "spends the summer as a guest instructor at the Thurn School of Art in Gloucester, Massachusetts. In the fall, [he] opens the Hans Hofmann School of Fine Arts in New York, which he will run until 1958."[25] In Walter Darby Bannard's work, *Hans Hofmann: A Retrospective Exhibition*, the opening date of the Hans Hofmann School is identified as 1934.[26]

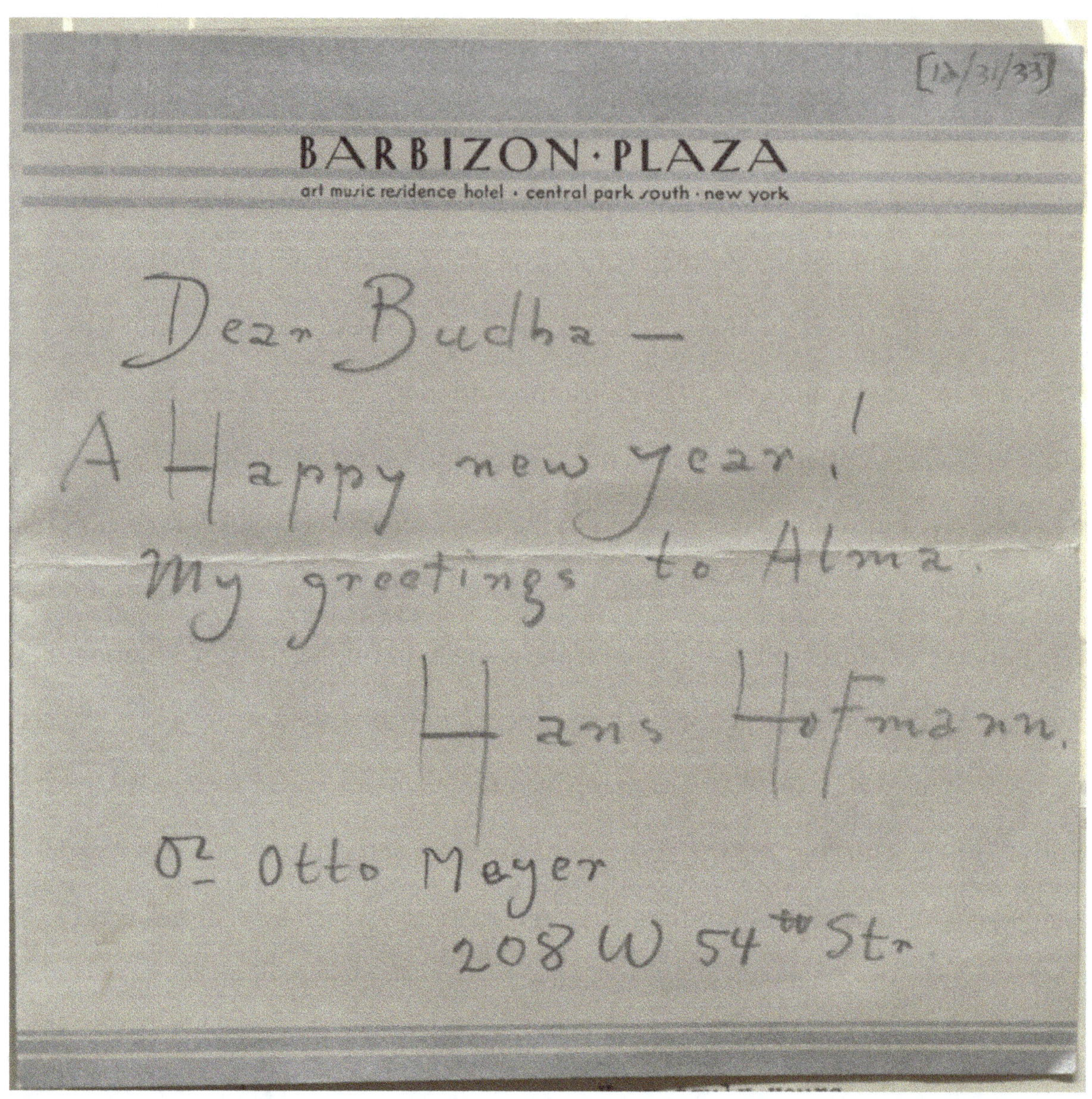

[12/31/33]

BARBIZON·PLAZA

art music residence hotel · central park south · new york

Dear Budha –

A Happy new year!

My greetings to Alma.

Hans Hofmann.

O.[o] Otto Meyer

208 W 54th Str.

Hans Hofmann's 1933 New Year's Card to Ray Eames, Kaiser Family Papers, Collection of Charles and Ray Eames at the Library of Congress, Part I, Box 280, Folder 7, photograph taken by the author

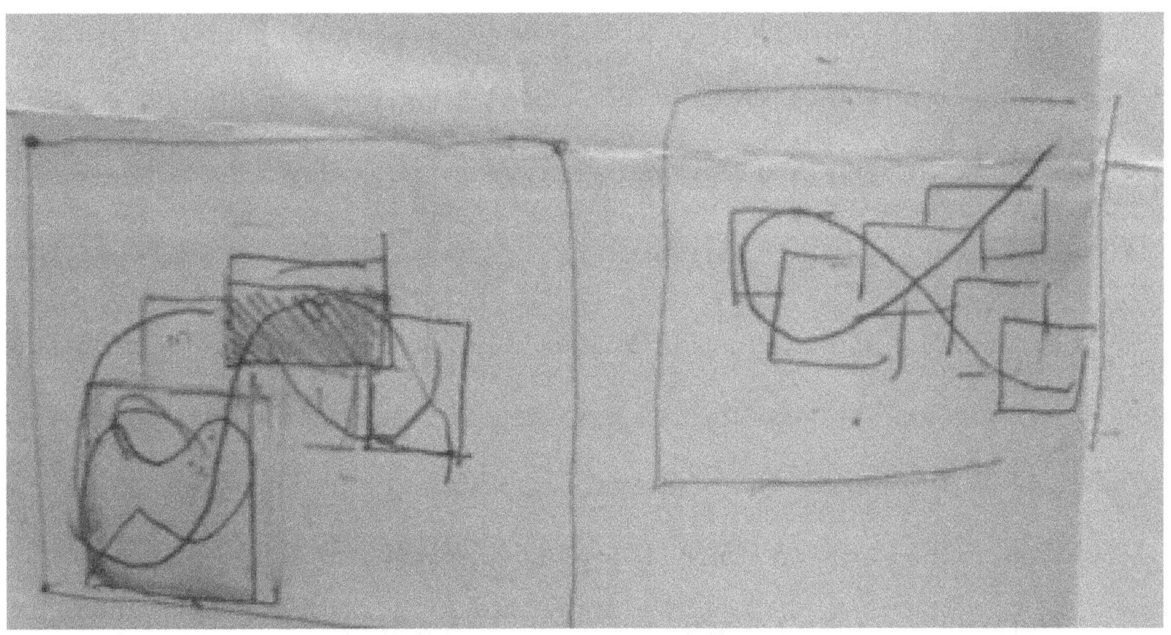

Sketches inside Hans Hofmann's 1933 New Year's Card to Ray Eames, Kaiser Family Papers, Collection of Charles and Ray Eames at the Library of Congress, Part I, Box 280, Folder 7, photograph taken by the author

Wilkin's 1933 chronology conflicts with the evidence in the Kaiser Family Papers in the Library of Congress, which support Bannard's 1934 date. On October 4, 1933, Ray wrote her mother a haphazard letter that reflects the confusion of her experience:

> What a day! Went to the studio after I left you and found that it had been changed to a Budgemon class! Saw Helen [a friend and fellow student] and we went in search of Hofmann—and found that he had left. We then went to the Barbizon Plaza—completely unstrung-and tried to get Hofmann—couldn't. Then I went with Helen to luncheon—No I didn't have any—I then called up Mercy [Carles]—and finally got Mrs. Carles who didn't know much. So Helen and I went to Macy's then I went back to the[…] at four thirty to meet Linda—found Linda who know nothing and we went to Tony's shop—a darling place—then went to Tony's apartment and who or rather whom should we meet but Mercy and Hofmann! *Had cocktails and he said he'd call me to have a talk with me before long—he is safe till February-when he'll have to leave but I think Tony is going to fix things up. I think Hofmann is going to have his own school somewhere—But I'm going to wait till I hear from him—and work here in my room.* [emphasis added][29]

In Ray's October 1933 letter, Hofmann's school has not yet been opened, and another letter in the manuscript collection also indicates that he taught at the Art Students League for part of fall 1933. Addressed to "Miss Ray Kaiser," from Anna Clarke, Executive Secretary of the Art Students League of New York, the letter is dated October 20, 1933. The organization's stationary includes Hofmann in the list of instructors. Clarke writes, "Would you be kind enough to inform this office by return mail the name of the class in which you have been studying at the League, due to the fact that Mr. Hofmann was unable to return to the school. If you have not been working in any class, we would appreciate it if you would inform us accordingly."[30] The source of all this confusion seems to have been the fact that Hofmann exceeded the limits of his temporary immigration period as he did not became an American citizen until 1941.[31]

Hofmann Establishes a School

In late 1933 or early 1934, Hofmann's school officially opened. Firsthand descriptions of the school and Hofmann's teaching style are often vague and fragmented. The Papers of Charles and Ray Eames contain a program saved by Ray from Lee Krasner's 1984 retrospective at the San Francisco Museum of Modern Art. Krasner was a fellow student at Hofmann's school in the 1930s, and Ray's lifelong friend. The exhibition pamphlet contains a valuable description of the format of Hofmann's school:

> [It was] organized into morning, afternoon and evening sessions. Students could be enrolled in one or in all of the sessions for as little as a week at a time. Morning and evening sessions were devoted to drawing from the model… while the afternoon session was a still life class. In his classes Hofmann stressed relationships of color and of structure, as the basics of art. He emphasized the importance of rhythmic

drawing and of relating edges and planes to one another and to the surrounding space.

On Fridays, Hofmann gave formal critiques and a series of public lectures, generally based on the color theories of Matisse and the architectonic compositional ideas of Mondrian. Lee Krasner attended these classes and invited art critic Clement Greenberg to join her. Through Hofmann's lectures and classes, American artists learned a synthesis of the most advanced concepts combining Fauve color, Cubist space and design, and Expressionist gesture and improvisation.[32]

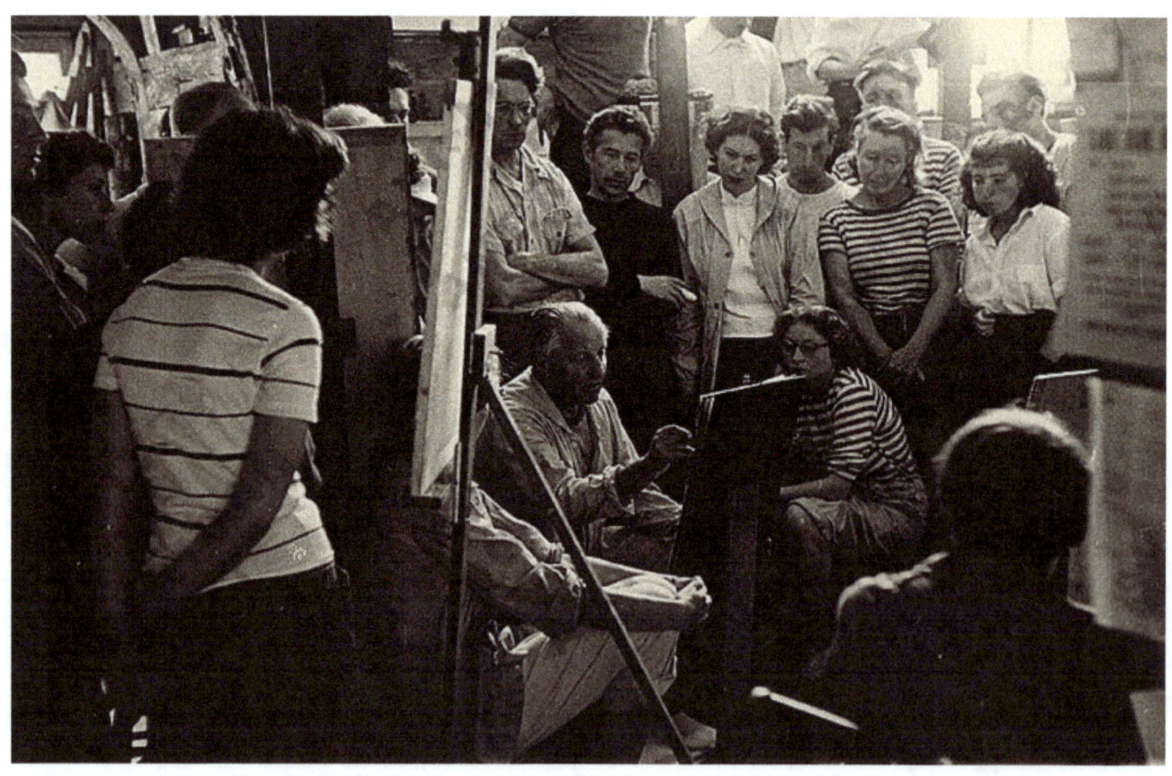

Class at the Hans Hofmann School of Fine Arts, Provincetown, ca. 1945 / unidentified photographer. Hans Hofmann papers, [circa 1904]-2011, bulk 1945-2000. Archives of American Art, Smithsonian Institution

An admittedly biased but fascinating picture of how Hofmann was possibly seen in his time is preserved in a 1935 advertisement for his Provincetown, Massachusetts school:

> Hofmann's value as a teacher lies in his capacity to follow his own great experience in painting with an extremely clear analysis. In the same way he is able to make the student conscious of his emotional experience and to realize this experience through pictorial emotion.... The demand for his classes was so great that he has remained here since then to teach at the Art Students' League, the Thurn School in Gloucester and has now founded his own school in New York, where many Americans have found beside the ideal working conditions, the rare opportunity to be part of a sincere artistic development. The beginner is greatly helped by contact with a group of painters varying in their degrees of development, each working toward a mastery of their own individual problems. The inspiring association with Hofman [sic] himself guides the students to increasing artistic freedom through discipline.[33]

A quote by Hans Heilmeier in the pamphlet reads,

> There are few that comprehend and are prepared to properly exercise the high authority which belongs to the true teacher. Hans Hofmann is one of these few. His criticisms are based much more on his clear knowledge of the essentials of Art and his own experiences in a life of artistic production than is usual with teachers. It is not alone knowledge, but the ability to see, to penetrate, to feel—that he conveys. He is rare in that his teaching is

> based on a great art experience, and he leads his pupils, as individuals, through problems of form and color, to pictorial reality of the highest meaning developed after timeless principles of vitality.[34]

Architect and designer Ben Baldwin described his experience in Hofmann's school for the Eames Office Video Oral History Project: "very often we were working in charcoal from a model and he would take a razor blade and slice the thing in lots of different pieces and move it all around, with thumbtacks, so that it had a much more spatial relationship…."[35]

Hofmann's Students

Hofmann is sometimes regarded, however unjustly, as more famous for the students he taught than for his own paintings. These students span several decades and include Lee Krasner, Helen Frankenthaler, Louise Nevelson, and of course, Ray Kaiser Eames. In 2003, PBS aired a documentary about Hofmann and his teaching narrated by actor Robert De Niro, whose parents were both Hofmann students.

Eleanor Munro, author of *Originals: American Women Artists*, describes the effect of Hofmann's classes on Lee Krasner:

> For Krasner, the most important sources would be Hans Hofmann's classes in drawing and painting, and the ideas of the Russian Surrealist-mystic John Graham. Hofmann… would influence two generations of American artists and critics, most of whom today are hard put to describe

the gist of a doctrine from which realist landscapists got as much as future Abstract Expressionists.... For Hofmann's classes in the late '30s, Krasner made dozens of charcoal drawings, plotting the lines of force of figures in standing or seated poses, carving the forms down to essentials with long, full-arm slashes and curves, pulling the farthermost reaches of the paper into the action with planes of rubbed shading.[36]

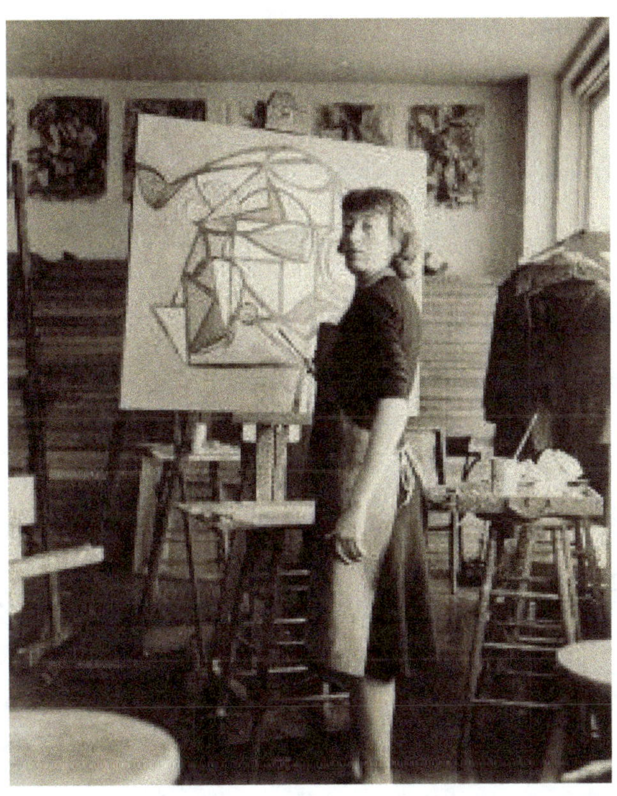

Lee Krasner, ca. 1938 / unidentified photographer. Jackson Pollock and Lee Krasner papers, circa 1905-1984. Archives of American Art, Smithsonian Institution

In addition to painters and other visual artists, Hofmann was unusual in that he welcomed students from a broad range of fields beyond painting. Ray described this phenomenon in the 1980 interview with Ruth Bowman:

"…my friend [Ben Baldwin], who was an architect and had also studied with Hofmann—as you know or might not know, many people studied with him who were not painters: sculptors, writers, musicians, and architects all studied with him, and yes, what else is there—dancers. I can't think of all the different areas…. the point of view for him could be translated—I'm trying to think of someone similar, because I don't think that many of the people that we know as great painters are such great teachers. He really was."[37]

The multi-disciplinary interests of Hofmann's students are an intriguing factor to keep in mind when considering Ray's later career. Ray is often characterized as a painter who stopped painting (as can be seen in the title of the PBS documentary *Charles and Ray Eames: The Architect and the Painter* and in her oft-cited quote "I never gave up painting, I just changed my palette"). When Ray's later career is placed in context with the broader group of Hofmann's students, which included a diverse mix of architects, dancers, and musicians, her portfolio of furniture design, film, architecture, and exhibition curation is not at all surprising or out of place with the philosophical backbone of Hofmann's teachings. Rather than being a painter who gave up painting, it is instructive to instead view Ray as a creative individual who always had interest in artistic expression through a wide range of mediums, painting being just one of them. In Hofmann she found a teacher and mentor whose creative outlook matched her voracious interests, and she applied his lessons about the relationships between things throughout her career. As Gregory Ain, an Eames Office engineer from 1943 to 1945, said in a statement quoted in an essay by Eames expert Daniel Ostroff published on the Eames Office website, "Ray was able to 'bring things into relation with one another,' and to 'find the inner order in whatever she touched.'"[38]

The appreciation of Hofmann's students (and their assimilation of his teachings) can be seen in song composed during a Gloucester session, to be sung "To the Tune of 'Ach Du Lieber Augustine.'" The lyrics to the student composition read in part:

"Here's to Herr Hoffman [sic]
Our teacher so famous
Here's to Herr Hoffman
Oh long may he live.
To teach us of volumes
Of tensions and rhythms
Here's to Herr Hoffman
Our teacher so rare.
He shows us what art is
And rightly does train us
To see the subtle difference
In dimensions two and three.
He teaches us space
That is swinging with movement.

It sways and resounds

Tho it may seem but air."[39]

Ray's Work with Hofmann

The majority of Ray's work done during her study with Hofmann was lost in storage, but interviews with two of her friends document the nature of this missing art.[40] Ben Baldwin recounted his memories of Ray's work with Hofmann: "He was very fond of her and very fond of her work. But it was very different from everybody else's in the class. There was nobody doing anything like what she was doing.... Her work was always very recognizable and not completely abstract. But still, it had the Hofmann stamp in that it had this spatial business that he was so adamant about."[41] Mercedes Carles Matter echoes Baldwin's statement, stating, "She had a character all her own in painting, a sort of arabesque quality."[42]

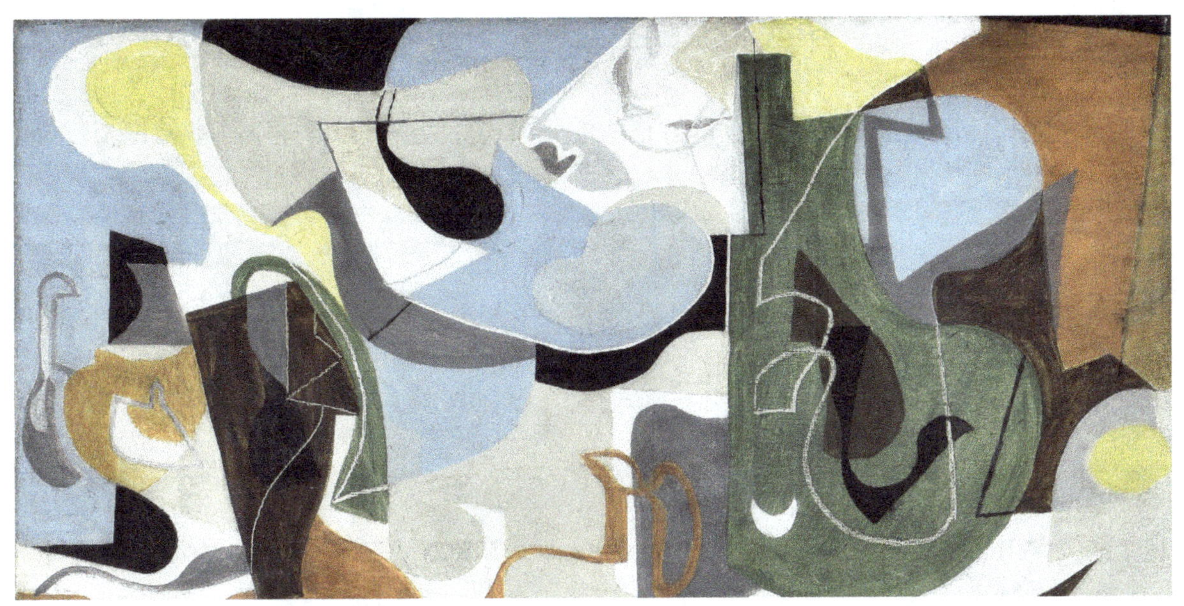

Ray Kaiser Eames, *Composition*, 1939, oil on canvas, 13 x 22 inches, Courtesy of The Columbus Museum, Georgia; Museum purchase and Gifts by Exchange of Mr. and Mrs. R.H. Wright, Estate of Frank J. Dudley, Mr. and Mrs. D.A. Turner, and Norman Rothschild G.2012.6

Hofmann's Teaching Philosophy

Ruth Bowman documented Hofmann's teaching style in her 1980 interview with Ray:

"RUTH BOWMAN: He lectured to you, while you were drawing, about generalities, or he had specific things to say?

RAY KAISER EAMES: No, he criticized each. I don't know how he did it later.... When I was there we drew and he would come to each person and criticize in relation to that person, you know. He talked about plasticity. If someone was beginning he never destroyed what that person had, he only enlarged it, but never cut down. If someone made a little tiny drawing on a big sheet of paper, he would never say, you know, that's not right—never anything about right or wrong at all—how to just increase what one felt. Each person would follow the criticisms and then evenings, or sometimes, every once in a while, whenever it was, he would have a whole lecture, give an hour or half hour—I don't know how long it would be—and there were many people who took notes."[43]

Ray's own notes from these lectures survive, many carefully recopied or typed. In the Bowman interview, Ray expressed her dissatisfaction with the published versions of Hofmann's lectures: "...most everyone cleans them up, and in the cleaning up the meaning disappears, as far as I'm concerned. Saying what he really meant to say—he had ways of saying things, just the word he would use, whether it was correct English or not, gave much more meaning, to me, than another word...."[44]

Hofmann's Teachings

A published version of Hofmann's "cleaned-up" teachings is *Search for the Real and Other Essays,* a collection of Hofmann lectures edited by Sara T. Weeks and Bartlett H. Hayes, Jr. In the title essay, "The Search for the *Real* in Visual Art," Hofmann proclaims,

> The artist's technical problem is how to transform the material with which he works back into the sphere of the spirit.
>
> This two-way transformation proceeds from metaphysical perceptions, for metaphysics is the *search* for the essential nature of reality. And so artistic creation is the metamorphosis of the external physical aspects of a thing into a self-sustaining spiritual reality. Such is the magic act which [sic] takes place continuously in the development of a work of art. On this and only on this is creation based.[45]

One of Hofmann's key concepts was the use of what he called push/pull forces to create depth instead of the established technique of vanishing point perspective. This philosophy is explained in "The Search for the *Real*": "*Push and pull* are expanding and contracting forces which [sic] are activated by carriers in visual motion. Planes are the most important carriers, lines and points less so. The forces of *push and pull* function three dimensionally without destroying other forces functioning two dimensionally."[46]

Many of Ray's papers are covered with paraphrased versions of this text along with accompanying doodles of push/pull planes, numbered rectangles that create the illusion of depth. Ray's extensive notes contain similar versions of many of Hofmann's published teachings but retain the idiosyncrasies of Hofmann's German-inflected English. Most of the notes of are hand-written, but one typed transcript is entitled "Notes on Hofmann's Lectures 'Buddha' 1933."[47] ("Buddha" was Hofmann's nickname for her).
An excerpt reads,

"A picture plane is two dimensional, free of depth. Nature is three dimensional, but the appearance of nature is two dimensional.

The period of Expressionism, from a literary standpoint, was psychological—the artist expressing himself. We ask more today, nature must be expressed in a pure way in relation to the picture plane, must create a depth but in the end it must be two dimensional, no holes.

Only in experiencing nature in the highest three dimensionality can we create the two dimensional.

Positive and negative space important.

Anatomy and perspective "rien" [sic]. Perspective is opposite of true art turns it intellectual.

Art is purely emotion but must be controlled. Children work only emotionally, beautiful, but not art. Our work has to have a basis, must have construction, but something over the construction."[48]

In response to Ruth Bowman's question, "What was the most important thing you think you got from Hofmann?" Ray answered,

> I have no idea of what it would be like to just suddenly come upon him, because, you know, over the years he was such a great friend and such a wonderful person to be with.... No one could enjoy anything more than he, but as far as his teaching, I think it was structure and relationships, and color as structure, and afterward I read theories that just make my skin crawl, they frighten me so, it's "fixing things," saying what he meant. What he meant just had nothing to do with, to me, fixing things in little boxes. That is the opposite to what he said. He didn't close anything, he opened everything and made it possible to see wholly, I think, as we do see. We don't see a line, we see a line and both sides of the line. It took his large view to make it possible for all of us to see and feel and know more. I don't know other teachers, I don't know of anyone who was as able to relate the experience of life to a canvas, to a format.[49]

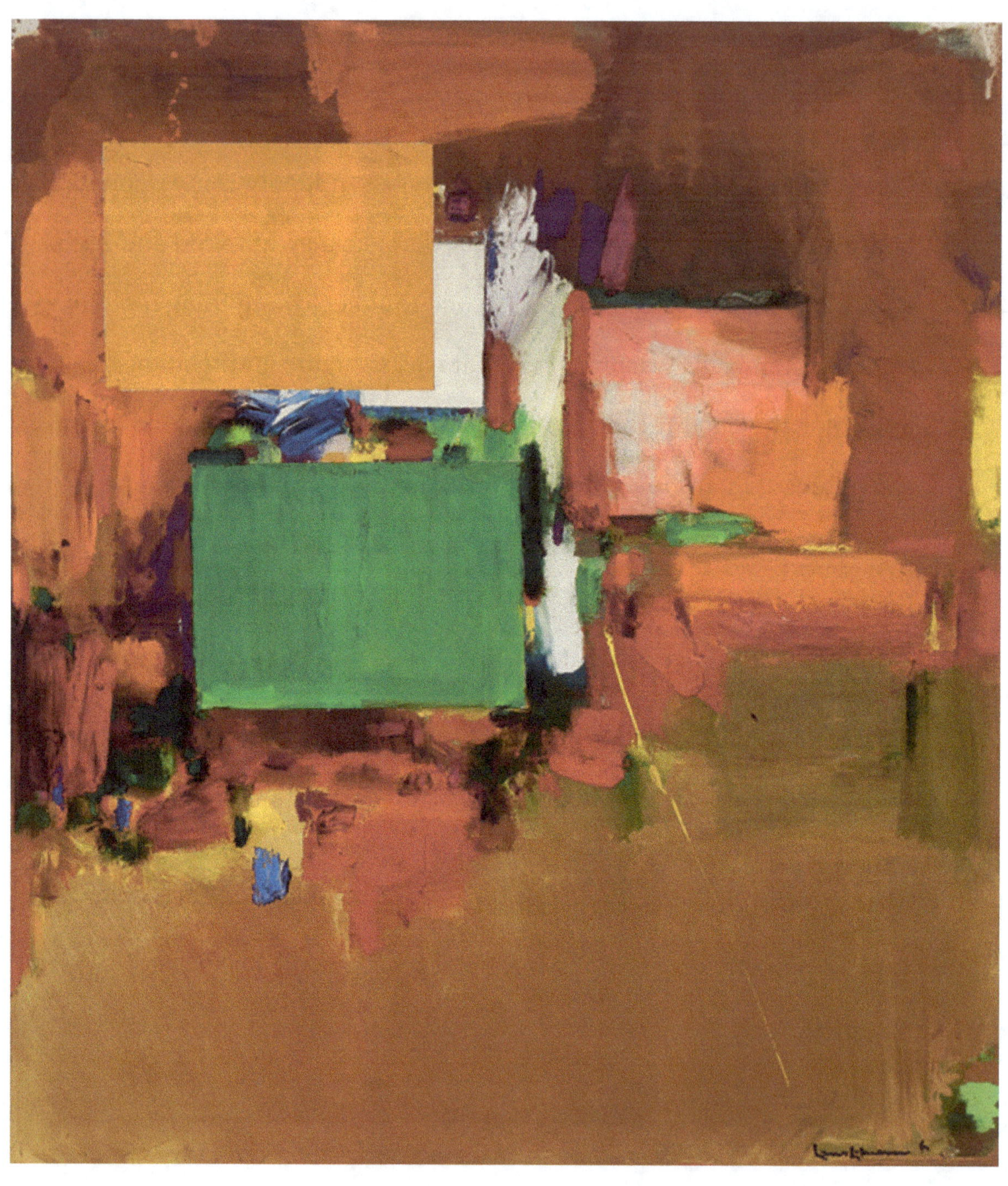

Hans Hofmann (German, 1880-1966), "Song of the Nightingale," oil on canvas, 1964, Private Collection, WikiArt fair use image

Hofmann's Work

The distinction between Hofmann's careers as a teacher and painter was clear-cut. Although Ray later had Hofmann paintings displayed in her home in California, she most likely did not see examples of his work during her study with him. Hofmann was careful to never let his students see his own work. Goodman writes "… it was 1943 by the time one of Hofmann's paintings was on public view in New York…. Until this time he had allowed only a few close friends to visit his studio, a restriction he attributed to fear that his students might not develop independently if they saw his work. His hesitation was, in fact, justified: once Hofmann's paintings were publicly available, so many of his students slavishly copied them that Leo Steinberg dubbed their readily identifiable style "Hofmannerism."[50]

Art historian Irving Sandler writes in an introductory essay to Hans Hofmann, The Years 1947-1952, "As [Hofmann] evidently saw it, his purpose was to synthesize compacted Cubist drawing with explosive Fauve color and paint handling…. Not only would he attempt a grand synthesis of the major tendencies of modern art, but… the assimilation of all that he could of his post-Parisian experiences. Almost from the start of his career, Hofmann was a radical artist, and he remained one to the end."[51] Hofmann did not work in one fixed style throughout his life. Early works are Impressionist while others are infused with Cubism. Sandler writes, "Hofmann himself had discovered two radically new ways of by-passing Cubism, both of which he would continue to develop until the end of his life. One was to compose abstractions from splashed and dribbled areas of pigment whose running edges looked random and uncontrolled—this as early as 1944, three years before Jackson Pollock began his 'drip' painting."[52]

Wilkin states Hofmann and Pollock had known each other since 1942, when Lee Krasner introduced them.[53] The Estate of Hans Hofmann adds further in their Hofmann chronology that in 1942 Krasner and Pollock lived next door to him at 46 E. 8th Street.[54]

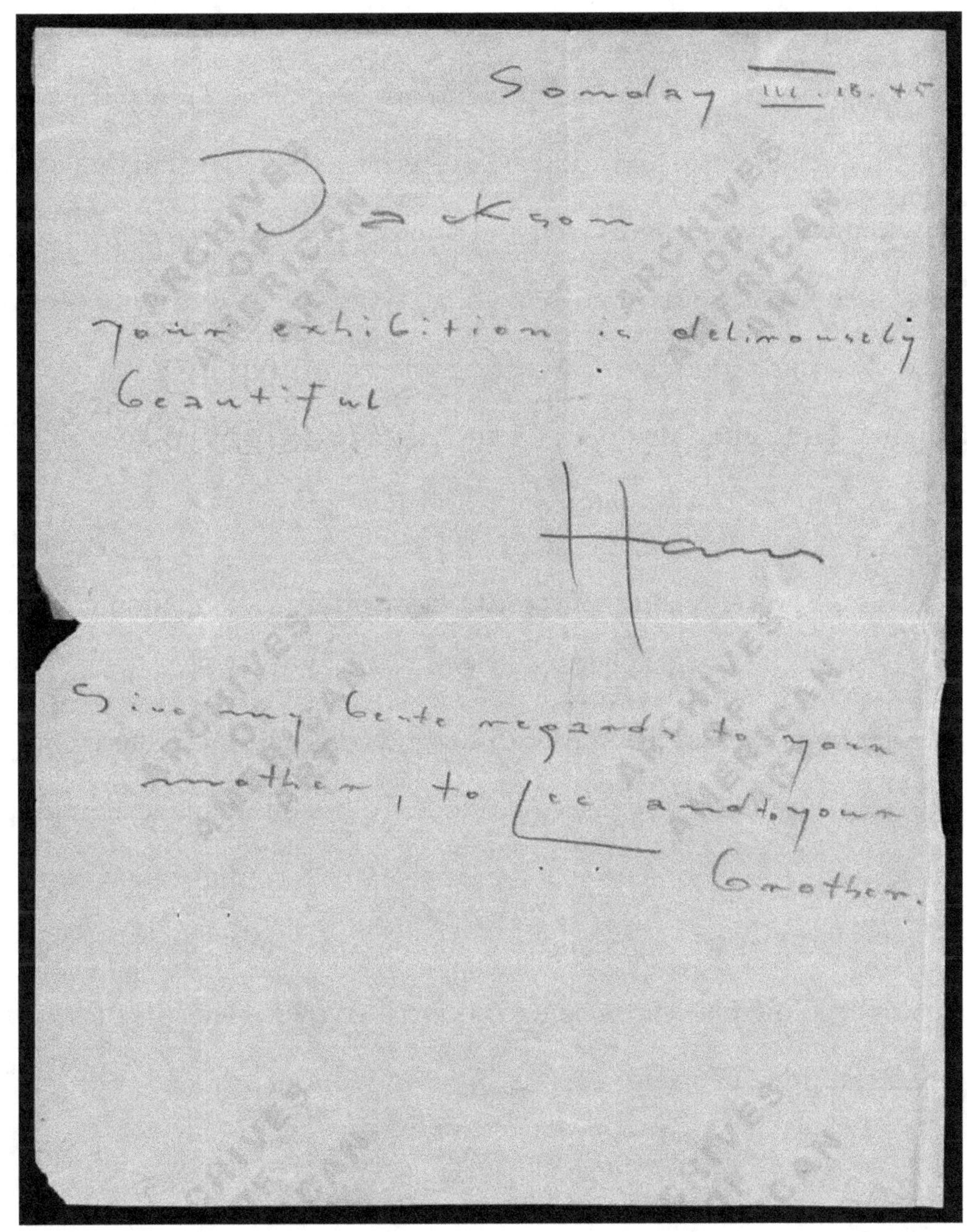

Sonday III.18.45

Jackson

your exhibition is delirousely beautiful

Hans

Give my beste regards to your mother, to Lee and to your brother.

March 18, 1945 letter from Hans Hofmann to Jackson Pollock, complimenting him on his "deliriously beautiful" exhibition and asking him to give his best regards to Lee Krasner and Pollock's mother and brother, Jackson Pollock and Lee Krasner Papers, Archives of American Art, Smithsonian Institution.

Despite the stylistic variety of Hofmann's work, there are elements common to many of his paintings. Hofmann applied his mediums in a painterly fashion, with thick impasto and spontaneous gestures. A spiritual quality permeates many of his works, as well as a sense of power that recalls the Romantics' concept of the sublime. His colors reflect the Fauve influence Sandler mentioned. They are often rich and searing, placed in unusual combinations. Hofmann's distinctive colors are a result of his philosophy about the role of color in art. As he stated in a published essay,

> ... The reciprocal relation of color to color produces a phenomenon of a more mysterious order. This new phenomenon is psychological. A high sensitivity is necessary in order to expand color into the sphere of the surreal without losing creative ground. Color stimulates certain moods in us. It awakens joy or fear in accordance with its configuration. In fact, the whole world, as we experience it visually, comes to us through the mystic realm of color. Our entire being is nourished by it. This mystic quality of color should likewise find expression in a work of art.[55]

Hofmann's Legacy

Hofmann's 1933 New Year's Card to Ray marks the early era of their relationship. The Library of Congress papers also contain a corresponding record of her affection for Hofmann, made years later. In 1938, Ray traveled to St. Petersburg, Florida to care for her sick mother. The file includes a "Railway Express Agency Uniform Express Receipt" dated Dec. 19, 1938. The package is for Hans Hofmann, New York, and was sent by "R.B Kaiser."[56] This slip suggests that a grateful student sent a Christmas present to the teacher who had influenced her work so profoundly. Given the tragic early death of Ray's biological father when she was a teenager, it is likely that Hofmann also functioned as a positive paternal presence in her life. In 1980 Ray fondly recalled, "he was marvelous. It was a great part of my life—a great experience. It meant a great deal to me. I worked with him for years. You know, it was like working with him, it wasn't as most classes are considered today, I think. It just went on and on."[57]

A brochure advertising the Hans Hofmann School contains a statement from the artist himself:

> There is much talent in America, as indeed there is everywhere. The whole question for the young artist is not to follow the prevalent ideas in art, but to absorb them to their full potentialities in order to have a clear point of departure from which, in future, to develop new directions. The forming of these will not only express the whole personality of the artist and mold his technique, but will be a true expression of American culture. To do this through work and struggle with the ideas representing our time—this is the modern artist.[58]

Ray developed these new directions Hofmann described in his hopes for his young artists in her subsequent design career in the Eames Office.

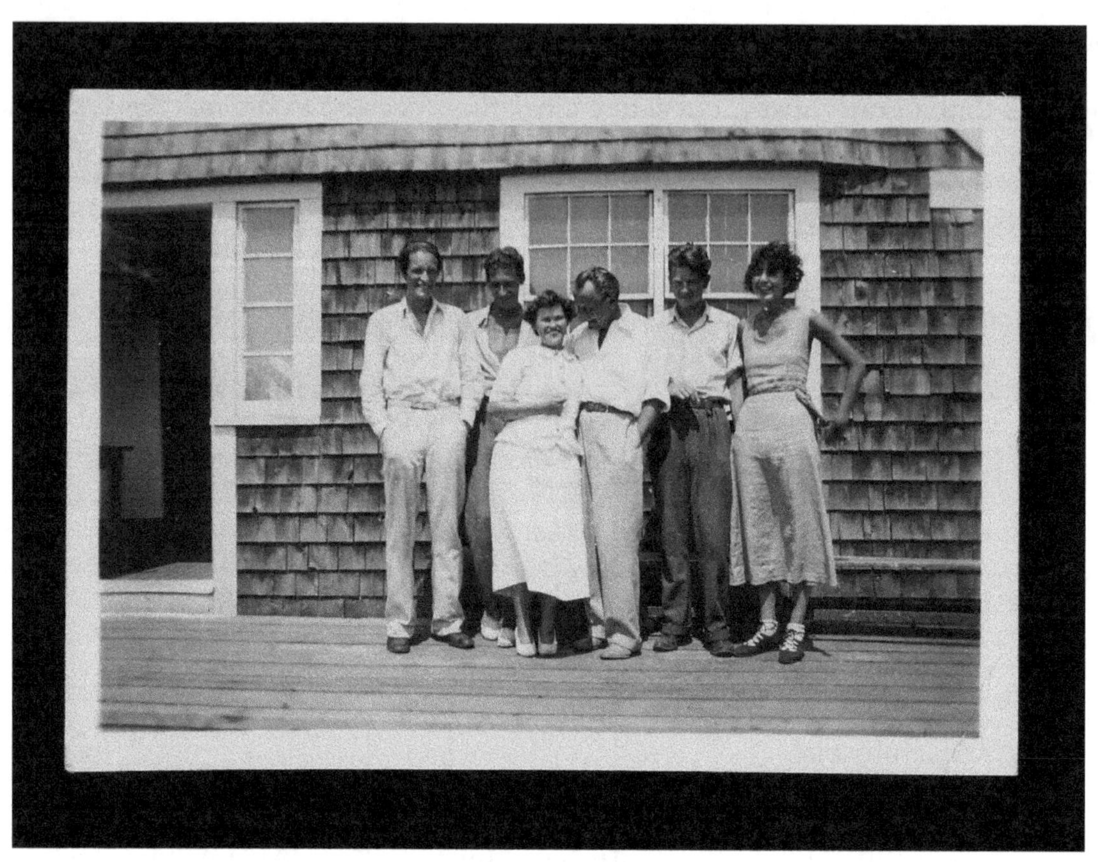

Hans Hofmann (center) with a group of students, likely at his summer program in Provincetown, Massachusetts in the early 1930s. Ray Eames appears to be standing next to Hofmann to his left, and the woman standing at the far right may be Mercedes Carles Matter. Hans Hofmann Papers, Box 9, Folder 30: Hans Hofmann with Students/Students, circa 1920-1950, Archives of American Art, Smithsonian Institution.

Chapter 3: Ray in New York City

Folder after folder in the Collection of Charles and Ray Eames at the Library of Congress is stuffed with programs Ray saved from her attendance at a profusion of New York City museum exhibitions, theater shows, concerts, dances, and films.[60] In *The Work of Charles and Ray Eames: A Legacy of Invention*, architectural designer Joseph Giovannini reveals that Ray's 1930s papers, including the programs, were originally stored in a trunk. Giovannini underscores the importance of studying what Ray saved as clues to her influences, stating, "At an especially rich cultural moment in New York, when traditional and modern art confronted one another head-on through artists who were often effectively activists, Ray was not only a sponge, every pore open, but also a brilliantly placed player in the course of events for the rest of the decade. The paper trail in the trunk documents a material biography of how she voraciously fed her eye and mind the most stimulating material of her intense day."[61]

The programs are roughly divisible into the categories of art exhibitions, theater shows, concerts, dance recitals, and films. Closer examination of these programs reveals both a selection of what cultural events were available to a young artist in 1930s New York and what Ray was particularly drawn to. Many of the themes explored in the events she chose to attend also appear in her later design work.

Art Exhibitions

The art exhibitions span a wide range of topics. Within one month in 1936, Ray attended a show of "Old African Sculpture and Works of the Insane," an exhibition of "Women in Modern Art" featuring Anni Albers, Lillian Olinsky and Ray's friend Mercedes Carles, and a show of mobiles by Alexander Calder. Those three shows were just a few of the many she attended in that time period—there are eighty-one extant programs to art exhibitions from the years 1930 to 1939 in the papers of Charles and Ray Eames.[62]

From this chaos of visual stimulus, patterns and inclinations begin to emerge. Ray's perspective as a sculptor as well as a painter is evident in her propensity for sculpture exhibitions, which include a show of Wilhelm Lehmbruck and Aristide Maillol's sculpture at the Museum of Modern Art, "Constructions in Space" by Naum Gabo at the Julien Levy Gallery, two separate Calder exhibitions, both at the Pierre Matisse Gallery, another Lehmbruck show at the Marie Harriman Gallery, Charles Despiau at the Buchholz Gallery, Constantin Brancusi at the Brummer Gallery, and a slide lecture by Warren Cheney of Mills College on "Abstractionism Versus Expressionism in Sculpture" held at the Hans Hofmann School.

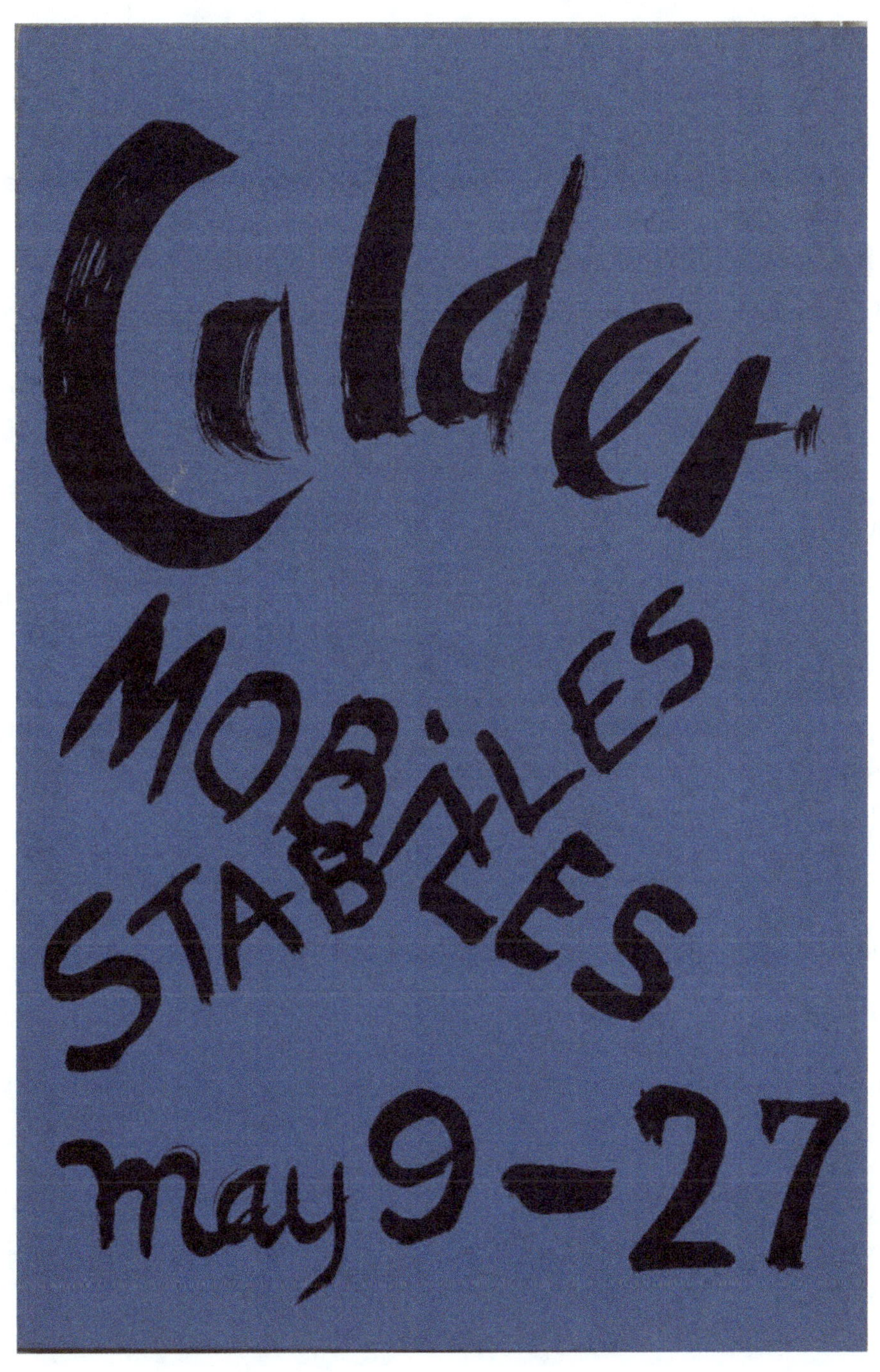

Alexander Calder exhibition program. Photograph of program by the author. Kaiser Family Papers, Papers of Charles and Ray Eames at the Library of Congress Part I, Box 283, Folder 1

The programs also reveal an interest in ethnic, folk and what was termed in the 1930s "primitive" art. Ray also attended "America/Oceania/Africa" at the Pierre Matisse Gallery, the "John Wise Collection of Ancient Peruvian Art," Crawford Shop hooked rugs at the Museum of Modern Art, and the "Hammer Collection of Russian Imperial Art Treasures" in addition to "Old African Sculpture and Works of the Insane" at the Midtown Galleries. The influence of Ray's attraction to African art can be seen in the Eames Office Time-Life stool, designed in 1960. The piece was directly inspired by two African stools in the Eames House. Ray and Charles acquired the African stools in a trade with their good friends the filmmaker Billy Wilder and his wife Audrey. In exchange for the stools, the Wilders received an Alexander Calder stabile (I think I would have wanted to be on that side of the trade!)[63]

Pat Kirkham writes, "Once Charles and Ray discerned the need for a small seat that could double as a resting place for coffee cups and magazines, it was but a short step to Ray's ideas of basing the new piece on the African stool they had at home, which they used as a "percher," a table, and a plant stand. The Time-Life stool is usually attributed to Ray."[64]

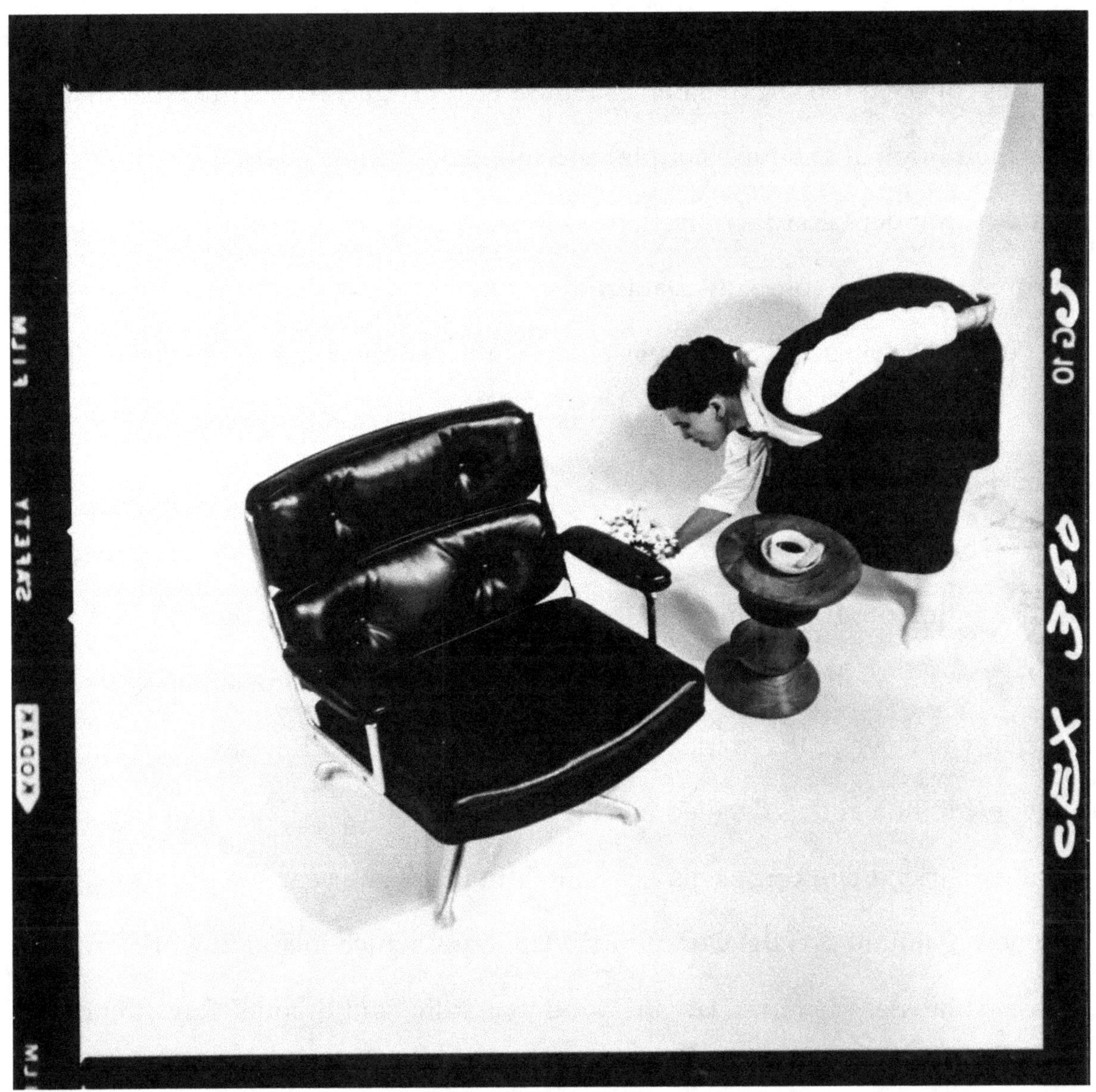

Ray Eames pictured with the Time-Life Stool. From the personal collection of Alexander & Vanessa Wendl; toad archive, (toadarchive.com), Photograph licensed by Eames Office, © Eames Office LLC (eamesoffice.com). All rights reserved.

Ray's interest in folk art also continued throughout her life. Ray and Charles collected folk art (the Eames House bird produced by Vitra is modeled after their original antique example) and followed the growth of their close friend Alexander Girard's collection. Girard, an artist and textile designer for Herman Miller, the company that produced Eames designs, amassed over 100,000 folk art objects.[65] Clippings about Girard's collections in the Eames Office files reflect a continued interest in his activities and awareness of attitudes toward folk art in America.[66]

The work of European artists, especially the modernists, are prominent in the exhibition programs. In 1936 Ray went to a show of works by Paul Cezanne, André Derain, Walt Kuhn, Henri Matisse, Pablo Picasso, Auguste Renoir, and Vincent van Gogh at the Marie Harriman Gallery. In 1937 Ray saw a Fernand Léger exhibition and as detailed in a letter to her mother, actually met Léger through a friend working as his assistant.[67] In that same year she went to "Modern Paintings" at the Durand Ruel Galleries, which included works by Zak, Picasso, Matisse, Vlaminck, Derain, Soutine, Utrillo, and Braque. Ray attended a solo Picasso show as well as viewing his work in numerous group exhibitions.

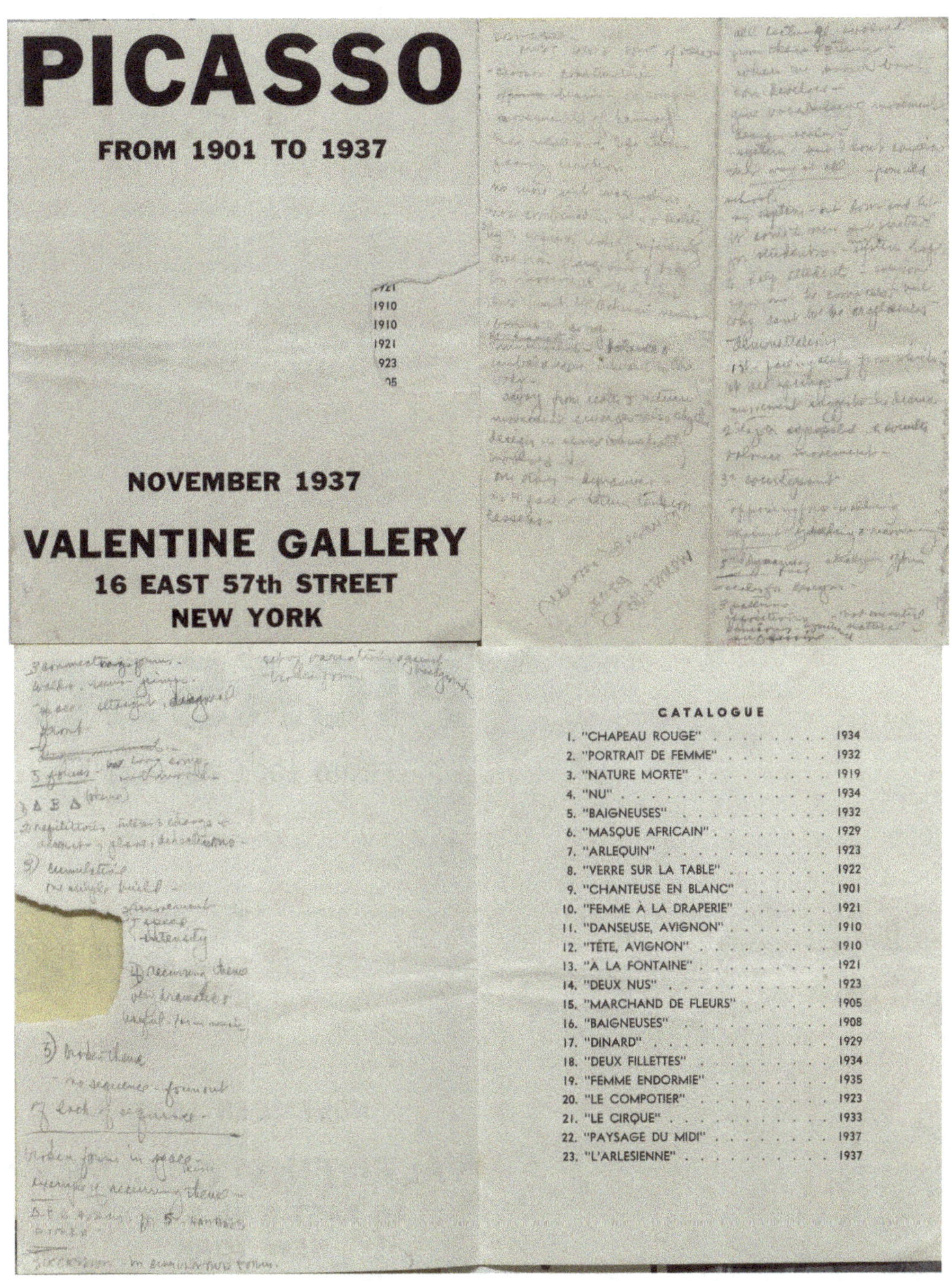

PICASSO

FROM 1901 TO 1937

NOVEMBER 1937

VALENTINE GALLERY

16 EAST 57th STREET

NEW YORK

CATALOGUE

1.	"CHAPEAU ROUGE"	1934
2.	"PORTRAIT DE FEMME"	1932
3.	"NATURE MORTE"	1919
4.	"NU"	1934
5.	"BAIGNEUSES"	1932
6.	"MASQUE AFRICAIN"	1929
7.	"ARLEQUIN"	1923
8.	"VERRE SUR LA TABLE"	1922
9.	"CHANTEUSE EN BLANC"	1901
10.	"FEMME À LA DRAPERIE"	1921
11.	"DANSEUSE, AVIGNON"	1910
12.	"TÊTE, AVIGNON"	1910
13.	"À LA FONTAINE"	1921
14.	"DEUX NUS"	1923
15.	"MARCHAND DE FLEURS"	1905
16.	"BAIGNEUSES"	1908
17.	"DINARD"	1929
18.	"DEUX FILLETTES"	1934
19.	"FEMME ENDORMIE"	1935
20.	"LE COMPOTIER"	1923
21.	"LE CIRQUE"	1933
22.	"PAYSAGE DU MIDI"	1937
23.	"L'ARLESIENNE"	1937

Ray's program from a 1937 Pablo Picasso exhibition at the Valentine Gallery filled with her handwritten notes. Photograph of program by the author. Kaiser Family Papers, Papers of Charles and Ray Eames at the Library of Congress Part I, Box 276, Folder 12.

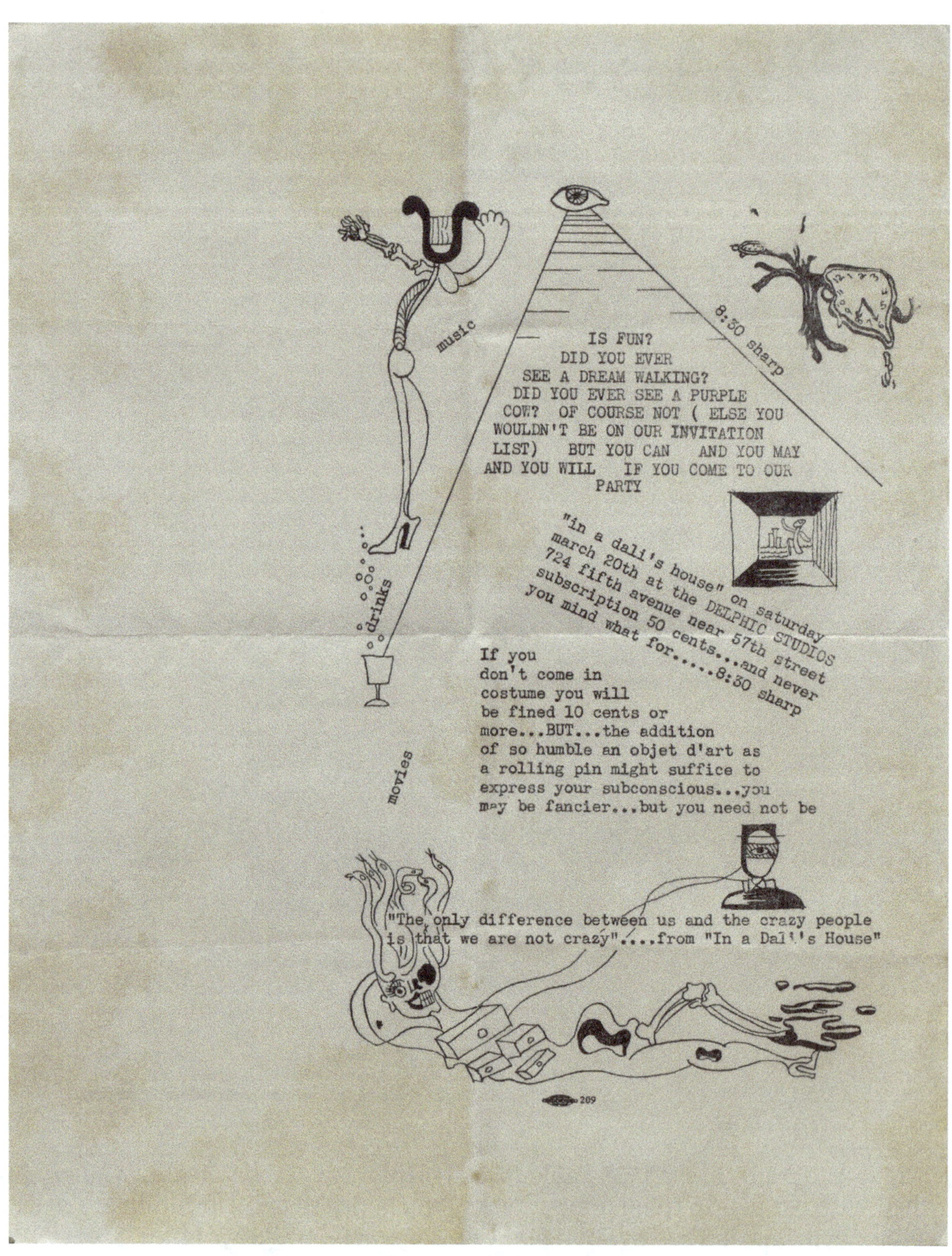
music

IS FUN?
DID YOU EVER
SEE A DREAM WALKING?
DID YOU EVER SEE A PURPLE
COW? OF COURSE NOT (ELSE YOU
WOULDN'T BE ON OUR INVITATION
LIST) BUT YOU CAN AND YOU MAY
AND YOU WILL IF YOU COME TO OUR
PARTY

8:30 sharp

"in a dali's house" on saturday
march 20th at the DELPHIC STUDIOS
724 fifth avenue near 57th street
subscription 50 cents...and never
you mind what for.....8:30 sharp

drinks

If you
don't come in
costume you will
be fined 10 cents or
more...BUT...the addition
of so humble an objet d'art as
a rolling pin might suffice to
express your subconscious...you
may be fancier...but you need not be

movies

"The only difference between us and the crazy people
is that we are not crazy"....from "In a Dali's House"

209

Invitation for a Surrealist event saved by Ray, photograph of document by the author, Kaiser Family Papers, Papers of Charles and Ray Eames at the Library of Congress, Part I, Box 276, Folder 11

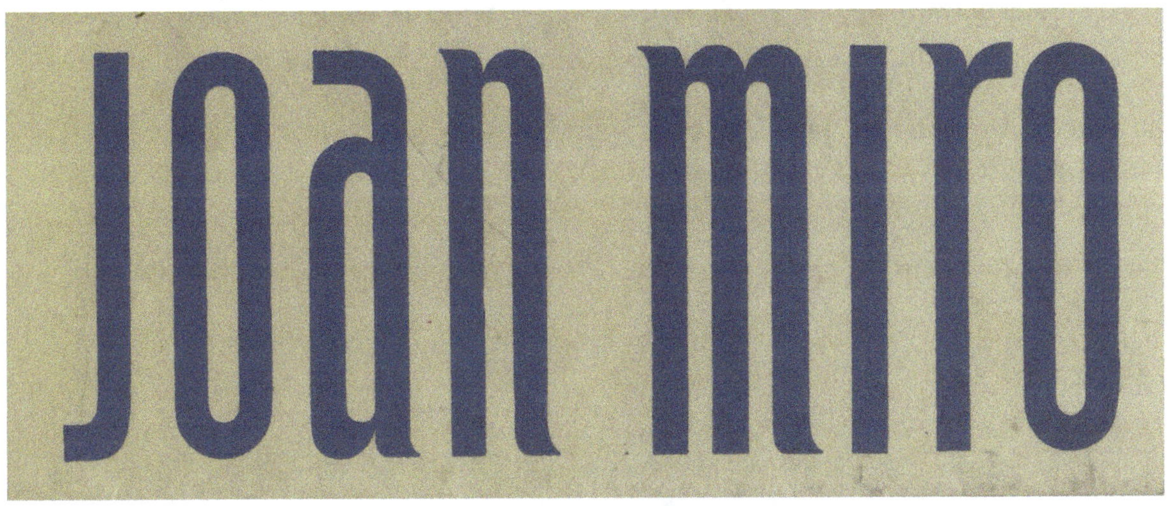

Joan Miro exhibition program. Photograph of program by the author. Kaiser Family Papers, Papers of Charles and Ray Eames at the Library of Congress, Part I, Box 283, Folder 1

Surrealism is another theme of the programs. Ray went to at least three Joan Miró shows, as well as an exhibition of Max Ernst.[69] The Ernst program is complete with its own Surrealist poem by Paul Eluard, which reads in part, "In one corner brighter for all the eyes/They await the fishes of anguish/In one corner summer's verdant coach/Stands gloriously and ever motionless."[70] Ray's interest in Surrealism is also evident in her newspaper clippings and letters.[71] She saved an advertisement for Surrealist shoes at Bonwitt Teller, the store where Salvador Dalí constructed his infamous window display.[72] Ray was not present at the event, but she notes in a letter that Hans Hofmann was.[73] Ray also saved a newspaper article on Salvador Dalí.[74]

The Eames Office files contain "study sketches and model photos of residences for Billy Wilder." A photo study for a door handle is composed in a distinctly Surrealist style.[78] The arrangement of objects is unmistakably influenced by Surrealism, and although it is not documented who created the assemblage, it is highly likely Ray was involved. Eames scholars have largely acknowledged Ray as the individual who was most often responsible for the compositionally beautiful arrangement of forms in the Eames Office projects.[79]

Theater Shows

Ray's father ran the vaudeville theater in her hometown. Growing up in an environment where she was constantly exposed to performances likely developed the love of theater suggested by the volume of programs she saved. A 1917 article from the *Sacramento Bee* in the Kaiser Family Papers boasts, "One of the things of which Alex [Kaiser] speaks with the greatest pride is the fact that he was the first vaudeville manager to pay Al Jolson $100 a week, then considered a fabulous sum."[80] While still at the Bennett School, Ray described a happy night spent on the subject of theater:

> Last night Mrs. Kennedy read the first half of Hamlet. You know, everyone has told me that's the best thing she does—her Masterpiece--- well you can imagine how thrilled I was last night. Then afterward we sat in the living room. *Just a few girls and the Kennedys talked for over an hour on Hamlet and then into [...] various tales of the old life of the theater. You know*

> *how that interests me.* It was ever so much fun. I wouldn't have missed it for the world. [emphasis added][81]

Ray went to plays by Eugene O'Neill, Gertrude Stein, George Bernard Shaw, Thornton Wilder, T.S. Eliot, Henrik Ibsen, Anton Chekhov, and William Shakespeare, as well as many by lesser-known playwrights. The files contain a program for Orson Welles' 1938 production of "The Cradle Will Rock," a famous work that became the subject of the 1999 movie *Cradle Will Rock*. She saw "The Cradle Will Rock" performed after the tumultuous incident. The program contains a telling interpretation of those events:

> Marc Blitzstein is one of the few composers who has qualified for biographical mention in this department of The Playbill. His debut as an actor came quite by accident last Spring. He assayed several roles in 'The Cradle' after the actors originally assigned to the parts became lost in the wilds of Times Square during that now legendary hegira from the Maxine Elliot's Theatre, where Federal Theatre officials refused to permit 'The Cradle' to open on schedule, to the Venice Theatre…[82]

There are several programs for Greek plays, an interest continued from student productions at the Bennett School. Ray saw "Porgy and Bess," Cole Porter shows, and Lawrence Olivier in a 1939 production of "No Time For Comedy" at the Ethel Barrymore Theatre.

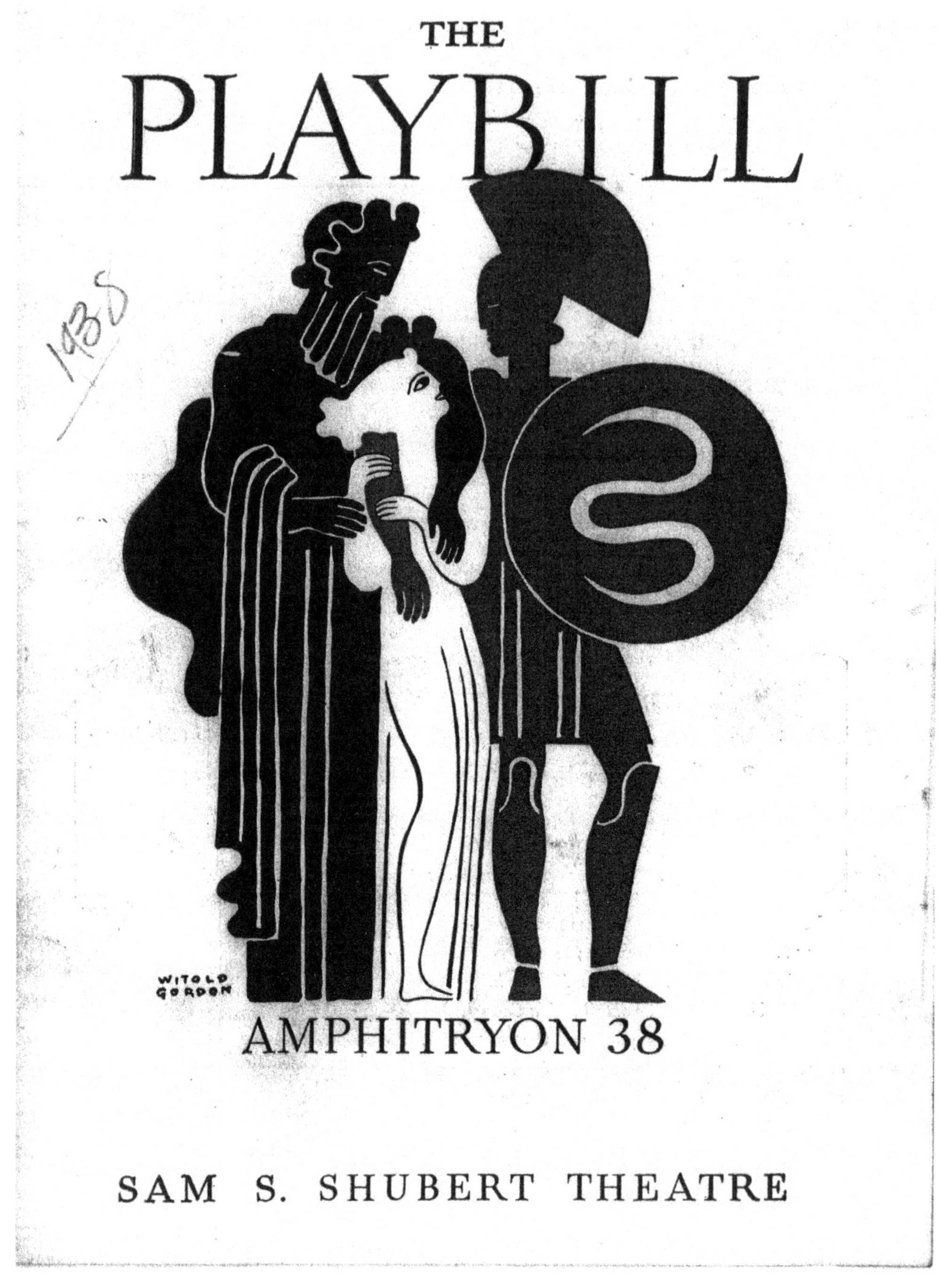

Kaiser Family Papers, Papers of Charles and Ray Eames at the Library of Congress, Part I, Box 287, Folder 3

She attended "Run, Little Chillun!" described as playwright Hall Johnson's attempt to "work out in dramatic form the community background in which... spirituals were born."[83] Ray's program to "Showboat" was autographed by actor Paul Robeson.[84] Her immersion in the world of New York theatre exposed her to many examples of stage design, costumes, and masks—all elements of the Eames Office work. Her analysis of Orson Welles' production of "Julius Caesar" reveals detailed observations about the set and production techniques:

"...it was beautifully done I thought—you know it is in modern dress and the whole thing seems so modern. The stage is completely bare except for a few layers on the floor (different levels) and the back is the back of the stage—white brick [...] the pipes showing! Of course the lighting is what makes it hold together—marvelous effects are gained from that bland wall—."[85]

Ray's close study of the art of performance and the logistical challenges of staging a production were training for the exhibitions and projects of the Eames Office.

Films

Ray's papers contain fewer programs to films than other types of cultural events, but this smaller representation does not prove that she went to films less frequently than other events. It is unclear how many film programs were produced and how many Ray kept. The film programs that do survive reflect her wide-ranging interests. The worlds of art and film are combined in a 1939 program where "The Museum of Modern Art Film Library / Announces / A Cycle / Of / Seventy / Films / 1895 / to 1935 / As Part of the Summer Exhibition 'Art in Our Time' / At the Museum of Modern Art."[86] Ray saw *Man of Aran,* a work by the famous documentary filmmaker Robert Flaherty, known for his film *Nanook of the North.*[87] *Man of Aran* focuses on a family living on an island off the coast of Ireland. Flaherty's innovative approach to documentaries may have influenced the inventive techniques that characterize the Eames Office films. Ray saw the 1936 premiere of Charlie Chaplin's *Modern Times,* as evidenced through the program and her reference to the film in the 1980 interview with Ruth Bowman.[88] Ray reveals that she saw the movie with Hans Hofmann: "we went to the movies and saw Chaplin in 'Modern Times.' I've never laughed more. He laughed so, we were just in stitches from it all."[89]

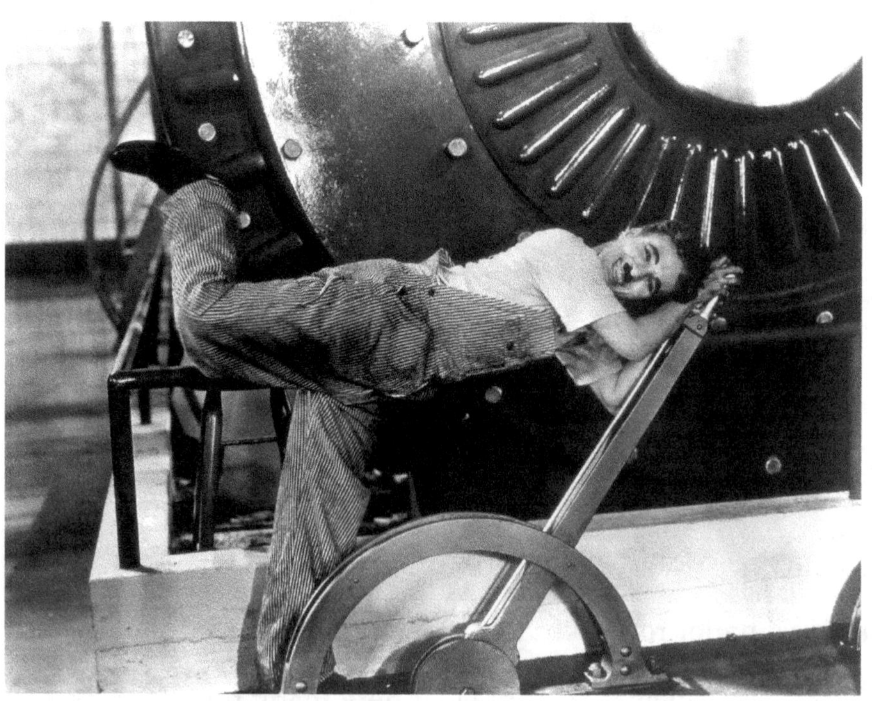

Publicity photo of Charlie Chaplin for the film "Modern Times" (1936), Public Domain image from Wikipedia Commons.

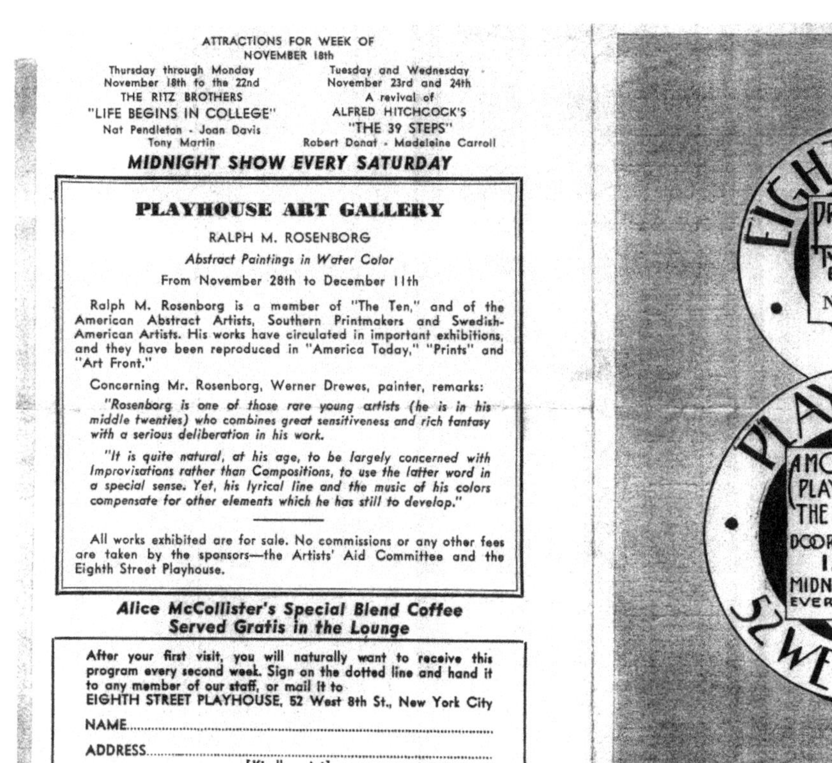

ATTRACTIONS FOR WEEK OF
NOVEMBER 18th

Thursday through Monday
November 18th to the 22nd
THE RITZ BROTHERS
"LIFE BEGINS IN COLLEGE"
Nat Pendleton - Joan Davis
Tony Martin

Tuesday and Wednesday
November 23rd and 24th
A revival of
ALFRED HITCHCOCK'S
"THE 39 STEPS"
Robert Donat - Madeleine Carroll

MIDNIGHT SHOW EVERY SATURDAY

PLAYHOUSE ART GALLERY

RALPH M. ROSENBORG

Abstract Paintings in Water Color

From November 28th to December 11th

Ralph M. Rosenborg is a member of "The Ten," and of the American Abstract Artists, Southern Printmakers and Swedish-American Artists. His works have circulated in important exhibitions, and they have been reproduced in "America Today," "Prints" and "Art Front."

Concerning Mr. Rosenborg, Werner Drewes, painter, remarks:

"Rosenborg is one of those rare young artists (he is in his middle twenties) who combines great sensitiveness and rich fantasy with a serious deliberation in his work.

"It is quite natural, at his age, to be largely concerned with Improvisations rather than Compositions, to use the latter word in a special sense. Yet, his lyrical line and the music of his colors compensate for other elements which he has still to develop."

All works exhibited are for sale. No commissions or any other fees are taken by the sponsors—the Artists' Aid Committee and the Eighth Street Playhouse.

Alice McCollister's Special Blend Coffee Served Gratis in the Lounge

After your first visit, you will naturally want to receive this program every second week. Sign on the dotted line and hand it to any member of our staff, or mail it to
EIGHTH STREET PLAYHOUSE, 52 West 8th St., New York City

NAME..

ADDRESS...
[Kindly print]

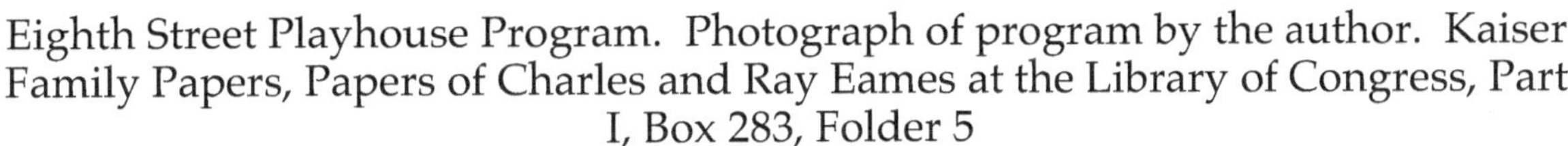

Eighth Street Playhouse Program. Photograph of program by the author. Kaiser Family Papers, Papers of Charles and Ray Eames at the Library of Congress, Part I, Box 283, Folder 5

Concerts

Ray's concert programs reflect a sophisticated taste in music and a thorough understanding of its structure. Many programs retain her scrawled notations of the scale structure. At a sonata recital of Jo Hawthorne on violin and Richard Malaby at the piano held at the Provincetown Art Association during one of Hofmann's summer sessions, she explicated the "Tempo de Menuetto" in the margins:

me me me me me re

re re re re la sol

do do do do me re

fa ti ti ti do.[90]

THE PHILHARMONIC-SYMPHONY ORCHESTRA OF NEW YORK

Conductors

ARTURO TOSCANINI

ERICH KLEIBER

BRUNO WALTER — 9 *want to hear him*

HANS LANGE, *Assistant Conductor*

ERNEST SCHELLING

Conductor, Concerts for Children and Young People

First Violins

very fine → M. Piastro, *Concertmaster*
R. Bolognini, *Asst. Concertmaster*
A. Lichstein
A. Gerardi
M. Muscanto
J. Fishberg
R. Henkle
M. de Stefano
D. Rosensweig
I. Strassner
R. Velten
G. Rabinowitz
A. Belfer
L. A. D'Amico
J. Gewirtz
A. Ribarsch
A. De Bruille
L. Busch

Second Violins

I. Pogany
A. Koszegi
F. Lowack
A. Dubensky
R. Heinz
A. Schuller
M. Dayan
S. Tomasso
A. Neveux
A. Lora
M. Borodkin
M. Kreiselman
R. Schenk
L. Sherman
L. Fishzohn
L. Dubensky
A. Stirn

Librarians

E. Greinert
N. Van Praag

Violas

R. Pollain
M. Cores
Z. Kurthy
J. Vieland
J. J. Kovarik
S. Lipschitz
B. Bardos
T. Fishberg
M. Tartas
W. Gray
M. Barr
G. Imparato
G. Harnisch
L. Verona

'Cellos

A. Wallenstein
J. Emonts
N. Dinger
W. Feder
A. Guidi
A. Bass
R. Stehl
V. Lubalin
M. Ormandy
O. Van Koppenhagen
H. Van Praag
M. Caiati

Basses

A. Fortier
H. Reinshagen
D. Rybb
E. Zickler
M. Tivin
M. Decruck
H. Jenkel
S. Levman
J. De Angelis
F. Zimmerman

Flutes

J. Amans
A. Ghignatti
J. Fabrizio
E. F. Wagner

Piccolo

E. F. Wagner

Oboes

B. Labate
E. Brenner
M. Nazzi
G. Apchain

English Horn

M. Nazzi

Clarinets

S. Bellison
O. Conrad
A. Williams
E. Roelofsma

Bass Clarinet

E. Roelofsma

E Flat Clarinet

A. Williams

Bassoons

B. Kohon
S. Kovar
R. Sensale
W. Conrad

Contra Bassoon

W. Conrad

Horns

B. Jaenicke
S. Richart
A. Schulze
L. Ricci
R. Schulze
M. Van Praag

Trumpets

H. Glantz
N. Prager
S. Klass
M. Schlossberg

Trombones

M. Falcone
A. Clarke
G. Lucas
R. Haines

Tuba

V. Vanni

Bass Trumpet

M. Falcone

Tenor Horn

M. Falcone

Timpani

S. Goodman
A. Schmehl

Percussion

A. Rich
S. Borodkin
R. Katz
E. Greinert
M. Van Praag

Harps

T. Cella
Miss S. Goldner

Piano—Celeste

Z. Kurthy
A. Schuller

Organ

Z. Kurthy

Transportation

L. Salter

Asst. Librarian & Baggage Master

J. J. Carroll

Manager Orchestra Personnel

MAURICE VAN PRAAG

Asst. Manager Orchestra Personnel

Henry Van Praag

Kaiser Family Papers, Papers of Charles and Ray Eames at the Library of Congress, Part I, Box 284, Folder 1

Jeanne Grover Evanston
1315 Wesley Avenue Ill.

SONATA RECITAL

JO HAWTHORNE, Violin
RICHARD MALABY, Piano

Provincetown Art Association

SUNDAY EVENING, JULY 28th
AT 8:45

I. Sonata in D major — G. F. Haendel
Adagio—Allegro
Larghetto-Allegro

II. Sonata in E minor — W. A. Mozart
Allegro
Tempo di Menuetto

INTERMISSION

III. Sonata in D minor — Johannes Brahms
Allegro
Adagio
Un poco presto e con sentimento
Presto Agitato

NEXT CONCERT SUNDAY, AUGUST 18th
Bach, Schubert, Strauss and Hindemith

Kaiser Family Papers, Papers of Charles and Ray Eames at the Library of Congress, Part I, Box 284, Folder 6

This sensitive appreciation of music extended to Ray's later collaboration with the composer Elmer Bernstein, who created original music to accompany many Eames films. Ray described the success of Bernstein's participation, stating,

> He understood when we've [Charles Eames and herself] always said we didn't want what's called 'Mickey Mouse' music, meaning, fitting to each movement. The music had to stand on its own, have its own structure. And so we would break down the structure of the film in whatever way we could and have these funny diagrams, and Charles would add what we called 'excitement curves,' and this would be calm and it would develop and it would be higher, then it would decrease, and either end strong or end quietly. So we'd have these lines on the charts, which Elmer understood perfectly.[92]

The genres of the concerts Ray attended divide roughly into opera, recitals of violin, piano, flute, and guitar, classical music, and ethnic music. Numerous programs exist for opera performances, including two separate Wagner works and a special fundraising staging of "La Traviata" at the Metropolitan Opera House to benefit Robert College, Istanbul, Istanbul Women's College, American College of Beirut, American College, Sofia, Athens College, Greece, International College, Izmir.[93] Most of these operas were at Carnegie Hall or the Metropolitan Opera House. Ray also heard violin, piano and flute recitals, as well as performances by guitarist Andres Segovia. The volume of programs for concerts by pianist Myra Hess indicates she was a particular favorite.

The evidence of Ray's exposure to classical music exists in the form of programs for Beethoven and Bach concerts. In a 1934 program, "The Philharmonic-Symphony Society of New York Announces a Beethoven Cycle Including All Nine Symphonies and the Missa Solemnis under the direction of Arturo Toscanini at Carnegie Hall."[94] In that same year, she went to "B. Minor Mass/J.S. Bach/(Complete)/Oratorio Society of New York/Carnegie Hall/Wednesday Evening, March 21, 1934/At 7:30 o'clock/(Thirty Minutes Intermission at Nine o'clock)/Albert Stoessel, Conductor."[95] The music of Bach would resurface later as the soundtrack to the 1952 Eames Office film *Blacktop: A Story of the Washing of a School Play Yard*.[96] Kirkham describes the start of the Eames Office's long relationship with Elmer Bernstein the following year: "The Eameses preferred their films to have original musical scores. Many of these were composed by Elmer Bernstein, who was fascinated by the relationship between visual and musical forms. The Eameses met Bernstein through a mutual friend. Because he was interested in both film and mathematics, they asked him to work on *A Communications Primer* (1953)."[97]

Folk and ethnic music provided a counterpoint to Ray's classical training. The files contain programs for Russian, Asian and Indian music performances. Ray heard Saveli Walevitch Russian & Gypsy Folk Songs and Clifford Vaughan Translations of Music From The Orient at the Barbizon Hotel.[98] At the New School for Social Research, she saw Sarat Lahiri and Todi in a recital of "Music and Songs of India/Authentic Presentation of the Ancient Music/Of India Played on Native Instruments/The Esraj/The Tabla/The Sitar/The

Banja."[99] A handwritten note on the program records the address of a place called the "Bengal Tiger."

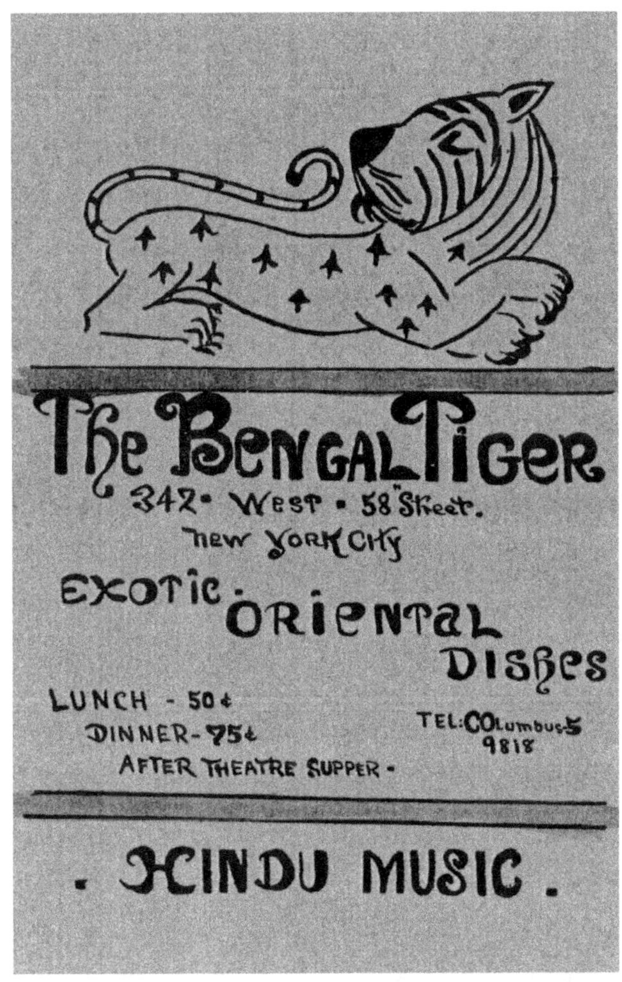

Kaiser Family Papers, Papers of Charles and Ray Eames at the Library of Congress, Part I, Box 284, Folder 6

Ray saw Sarat Lahiri perform again, this time with an individual named Loto. A quote featured on the program from *Vanity Fair* declares the pair is "More modern than the most determined futurists."[100] This program contains a printed card for the Bengal Tiger, identified here as an Indian restaurant. Ray's interest in Indian culture extended into the dances she attended in this time period and later became an ongoing subject in the design portfolio of the Eames Office.

Dances

Dance was an important element in Ray's life. As a child in Sacramento, Ray's parents provided her with the opportunity to study dance with teacher Leila Maple (a former member of the Russian Ballet) and during her time at the Bennett School and in New York Ray continued to take lessons from multiple dancers including Martha Graham, Hanya Holm, and Carmen Rooker.[101] Ray maintained a friendship with her Bennett School teacher Carmen Rooker through the 1930s and attended many of her recitals.

Ray voraciously attended dance performances. Unlike her widely varied taste in art exhibitions, plays and concerts, Ray attended the performances of a small number of dancers many times, many of them her teachers. These favorites were Martha Graham, Mary Wigman, Hanya Holm, Doris Humphrey and Charles Weidman, Carmen Rooker, the Ballet Russe, and Uday Shankar and his company. The extant programs are almost entirely for their performances. Exceptions include particularly notable dances, such as a recital by Anna Pavlova, and a presentation of three ballets by Igor Stravinsky choreographed by George Balanchine.[102]

Two benefit dances refer to international affairs of the 1930s. An undated program filed with papers from 1936 documents the American Bureaus for Medical Aid to China Inc. presentation of the Chinese Cultural Theatre Group in the premiere of "An Evening in Cathay" sponsored by The China Society of America.[103] On January 19th 1936, Ray went to "Dance for Spain/Benefit/Medical Bureau & North American/Committee to Aid Spanish Democracy," an event organized in response to the Spanish Civil War.[104]

Ray attended two dances sponsored by workers' organizations. An undated program reads "Workers Committee on Unemployment/Locals 2 and 3/298 Henry St./Presents/Nadia/Chilkovsky/In Recital of/Modern Dances/At/The Playhouse of the Henry Street/Settlement.... Paula Halpern at the Piano/We invite you to our meeting every Thursday night at 301 Henry Street./We urge you to join our struggles against hunger and evictions."[105] The second program is for a "Major Revolutionary/Dance/Recital/Workers Dance League/Program/Feb. 17, 1935/Center Theatre/Radio City/In conjunction with/International theatre week."[106] The content of Ray's letters to her mother in this time period do not indicate involvement in any specifically leftist groups. In fact, Ray's comment after seeing "The Cradle Will Rock" was "good music, but far too left—union—"[107] Based on the surviving documentation, she seems to have kept out of major political causes in this era. A lighthearted tone characterizes her description to her mother of a dance class she took: "...I'm going to dancing class in the morning—They are all communists in fact the class was arranged so as to keep the women out of work from mobilizing---Anyway I know it's good exercise cause Linda is stiff from it. Mercy [Mercedes Carles Matter] is also going."[108]

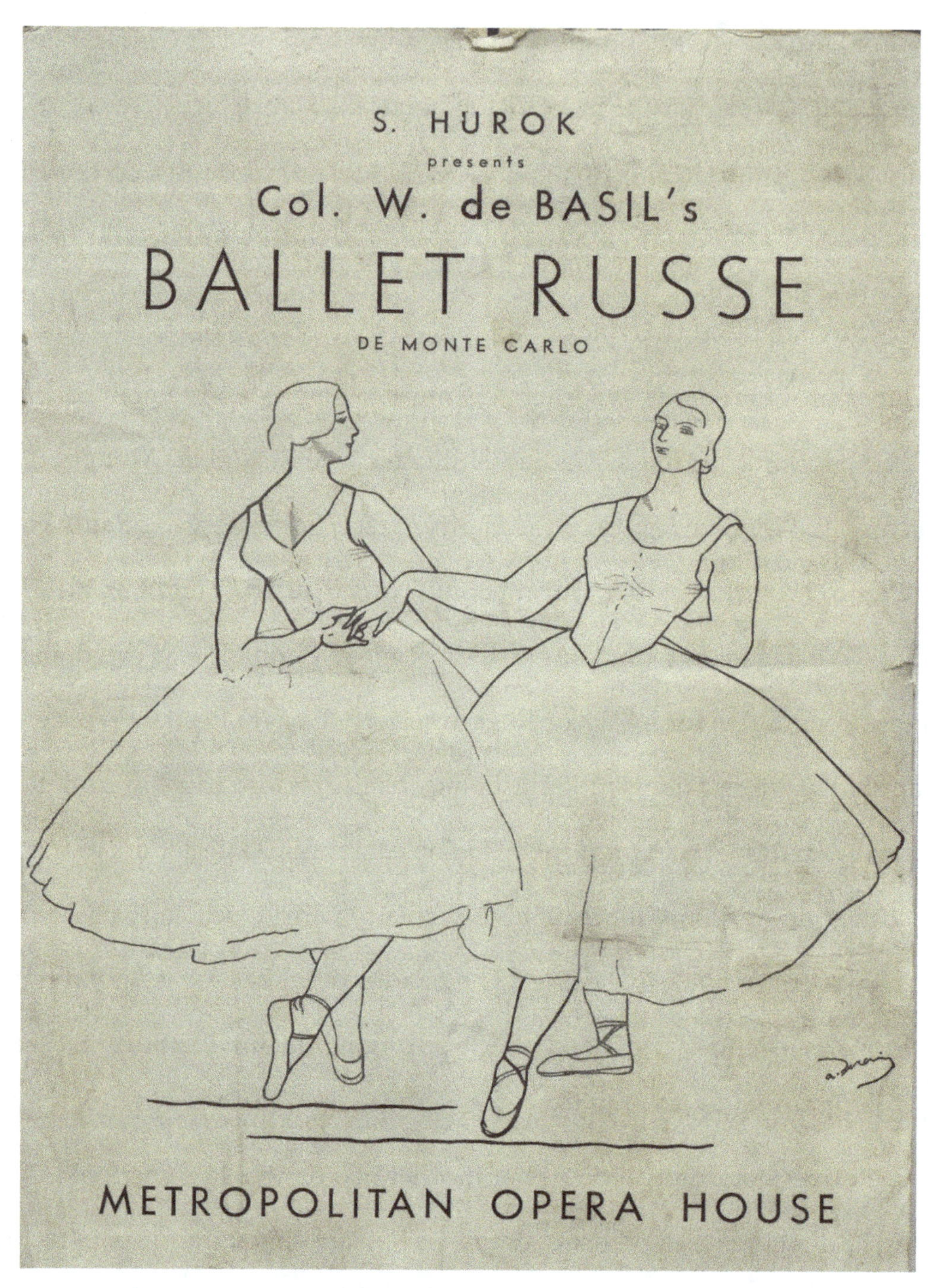

Kaiser Family Papers, Papers of Charles and Ray Eames at the Library of Congress, Ray's program from the Ballet Russe, Part I, Box 283, Folder 3

● THE AMERICAN BALLET

Presents Three Ballets by

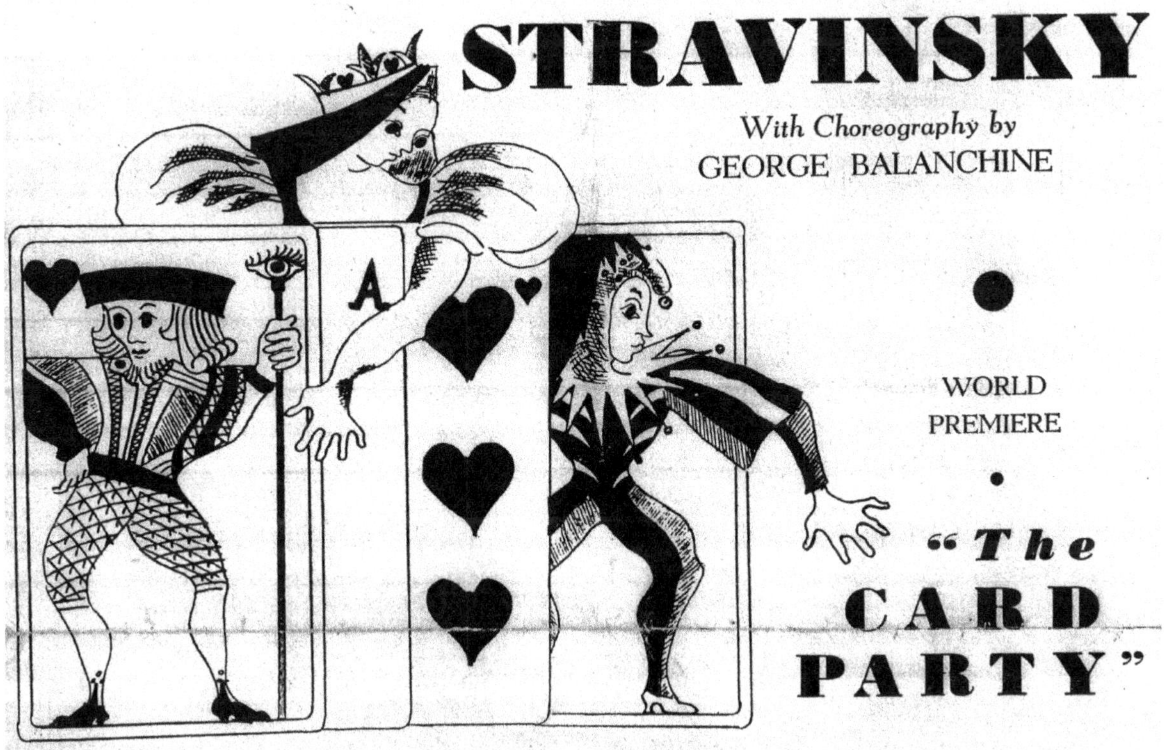

Sketch by Irene Sharaff

FIRST AMERICAN PERFORMANCE

● "LE BAISER DE LA FÉE"

FIRST NEW YORK PERFORMANCE

● "APOLLON MUSEGÈTE"

---

70 MEMBERS OF THE

● NEW YORK PHILHARMONIC-SYMPHONY ORCHESTRA

IGOR STRAVINSKY, *Conducting*

Tuesday and Wednesday, APRIL 27 and 28 at 8:30 P.M.

METROPOLITAN OPERA HOUSE

Tickets now on sale at Steinway Hall Box Office, 113 West 57th Street

Kaiser Family Papers, Papers of Charles and Ray Eames at the Library of Congress, Part I, Box 283, Folder 4

Ray saved six programs from Martha Graham dances. At least two Graham performances of modern dance she attended included artistic contributions from Alexander Calder and Isamu Noguchi. The program from March 1, 1936 reads,

> Under the general title 'Horizons' this is the first cycle of a suite built on the theme of Exploration and Discovery. While not specifically American, these dances are built on themes abstracted from the American background.
>
> The 'Mobiles' used in 'Horizons' are designed by Alexander Calder as a new conscious use of space. They are employed in 'Horizons' as visual preludes to the dances in the suite. The 'Mobiles' do not interpret the dances, nor do the dances interpret the 'Mobiles.' They are employed to enlarge the sense of horizon.[113]

The linkages between the worlds of fine art and dance are also evident in the program for a dance recital by Berta Oschner, held November 24, 1935. One piece was titled "Persistence of Memory" with a parenthetical note stating, "After a Canvas of Salvatori [sic] Dali." The piece "Legendry" is labeled "After James Joyce's 'Anna Livia Plurabelle.'"[114] Ray was a passionate admirer of both the work of Salvador Dalí and James Joyce, and her attendance at these dance performances synthesized her aesthetic and intellectual interests, combining visual art and literature and music with the physical act of dance.

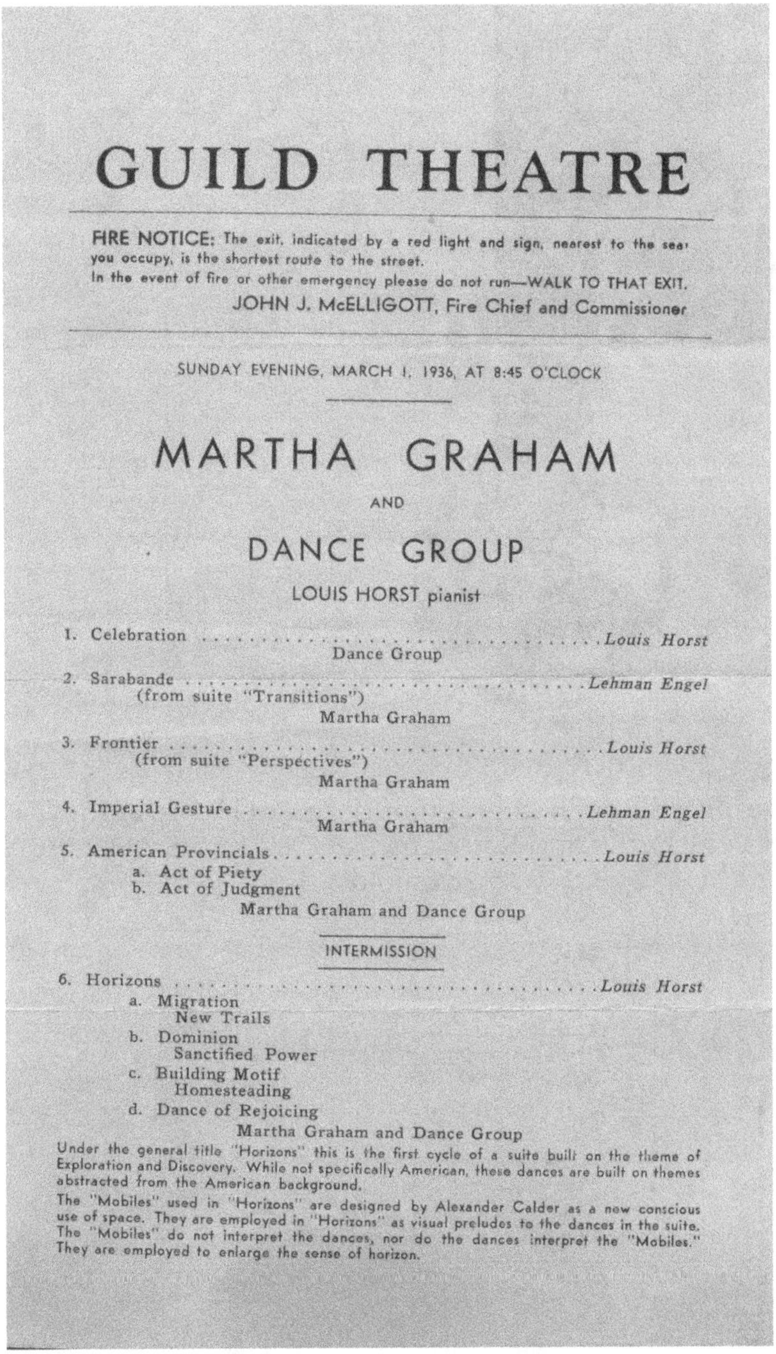

GUILD THEATRE

FIRE NOTICE: The exit, indicated by a red light and sign, nearest to the seat you occupy, is the shortest route to the street.
In the event of fire or other emergency please do not run—WALK TO THAT EXIT.
JOHN J. McELLIGOTT, Fire Chief and Commissioner

SUNDAY EVENING, MARCH 1, 1936, AT 8:45 O'CLOCK

MARTHA GRAHAM

AND

DANCE GROUP

LOUIS HORST pianist

1. Celebration .... *Louis Horst*
Dance Group
2. Sarabande .... *Lehman Engel*
(from suite "Transitions")
Martha Graham
3. Frontier .... *Louis Horst*
(from suite "Perspectives")
Martha Graham
4. Imperial Gesture .... *Lehman Engel*
Martha Graham
5. American Provincials .... *Louis Horst*
a. Act of Piety
b. Act of Judgment
Martha Graham and Dance Group

INTERMISSION

6. Horizons .... *Louis Horst*
a. Migration
New Trails
b. Dominion
Sanctified Power
c. Building Motif
Homesteading
d. Dance of Rejoicing
Martha Graham and Dance Group

Under the general title "Horizons" this is the first cycle of a suite built on the theme of Exploration and Discovery. While not specifically American, these dances are built on themes abstracted from the American background.

The "Mobiles" used in "Horizons" are designed by Alexander Calder as a new conscious use of space. They are employed in "Horizons" as visual preludes to the dances in the suite. The "Mobiles" do not interpret the dances, nor do the dances interpret the "Mobiles." They are employed to enlarge the sense of horizon.

Martha Graham program. Photograph of program by the author. Kaiser Family Papers, Papers of Charles and Ray Eames at the Library of Congress, Part I, Box 283, Folder 4

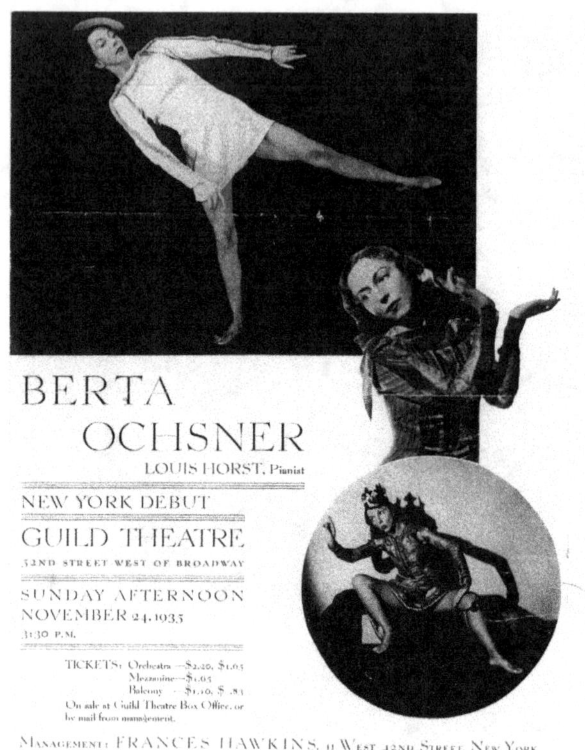

BERTA
OCHSNER
LOUIS HORST, Pianist

NEW YORK DEBUT

GUILD THEATRE
52ND STREET WEST OF BROADWAY

SUNDAY AFTERNOON
NOVEMBER 24, 1935
3:30 P.M.

TICKETS: Orchestra—$2.20, $1.65
Mezzanine—$1.65
Balcony—$1.10, $ .83
On sale at Guild Theatre Box Office, or by mail from management.

MANAGEMENT: FRANCES HAWKINS, 11 West 42nd Street, New York

P R O G R A M

1. Air and Sonatina . . . . Handel
2. La Lugubre . . . . Couperin
(Design for a Borgia)
3. Courante . . . . Chambonnieres
(The King Sets Forth the Fine Points of the Courante)
4. The King's Hunting Jigg . . . . John Bull
5. "Persistence of Memory" . . . . Robert Wolf
(After a Canvas of Salvatori Dali)
6. Whisky Johnny . . . . Jean Williams
(American Folk Theme)
7. Dove Cote . . . . Ernest Gillet

INTERMISSION

8. An Angel Dances . . . . Wolf-Ferrari
9. Comments . . . . Strawinsky
So What
Lament, Op. 1
The People's Choice
Exotique
Simian Quandary
Caliente
10. Legendry . . . . Hazel Felman
(After James Joyce's "Anna Livia Plurabelle")
11. Air . . . . Handel

Choregoraphy by Berta Ochsner

Costumes by Larene Marzolf Stone

Steinway Piano

Berta Ochsner program. Photograph of program by the author. Kaiser Family Papers, Papers of Charles and Ray Eames at the Library of Congress, Part I, Box 284, Folder 1

The dances of Uday Shankar and his self-described "company of Hindu Dancers and Musicians" were particularly effective in bridging Ray's interests. The files contain more programs for this group of performers than any other dancer. Uday Shankar was a dancer and choreographer famous in both his native India and abroad. Modern readers may also recognize him as the uncle of singer Norah Jones. In her repeated attendance of his performances accompanied by his "company of Hindu Dancers and Musicians," Ray received a thorough exposure to Indian music, dance, and culture, which remained one of her lifelong interests.

A program for the company's "Positively Farewell Performances before returning to India" (the third program in two months that advertised a farewell performance) gives an idea of the nature of an Uday Shankar presentation. It reads, "S. Hurok Presents / Uday Shan-Kar / And Company of Hindu Dancers and Musicians / With / Simkie / Kanuak-Lata Debendra Robindra / Positively Farewell Performances before returning to India. / Musical arrangement by Timir Baran Bhattacharyya (sarodist) in collaboration with Vishnu Das Shirali (sitarist and master drummer). All the dances are composed by Uday Shan-kar."[115] Ray took notes on the program, explicating the musical structure of the accompaniment to the dances.

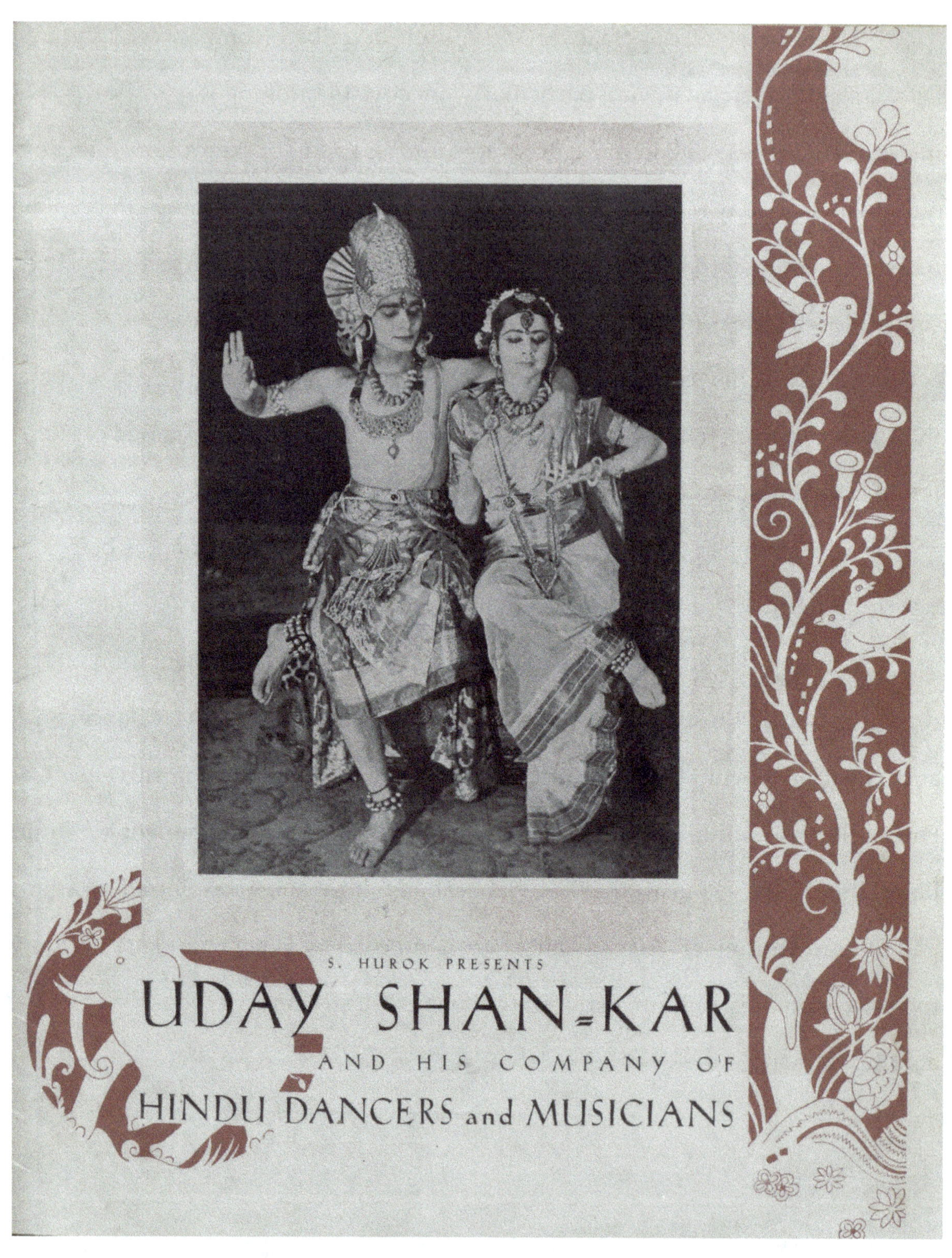

Uday Shankar program. Photograph of program by the author. Kaiser Family Papers, Papers of Charles and Ray Eames at the Library of Congress, Part I, Box 283, Folder 4

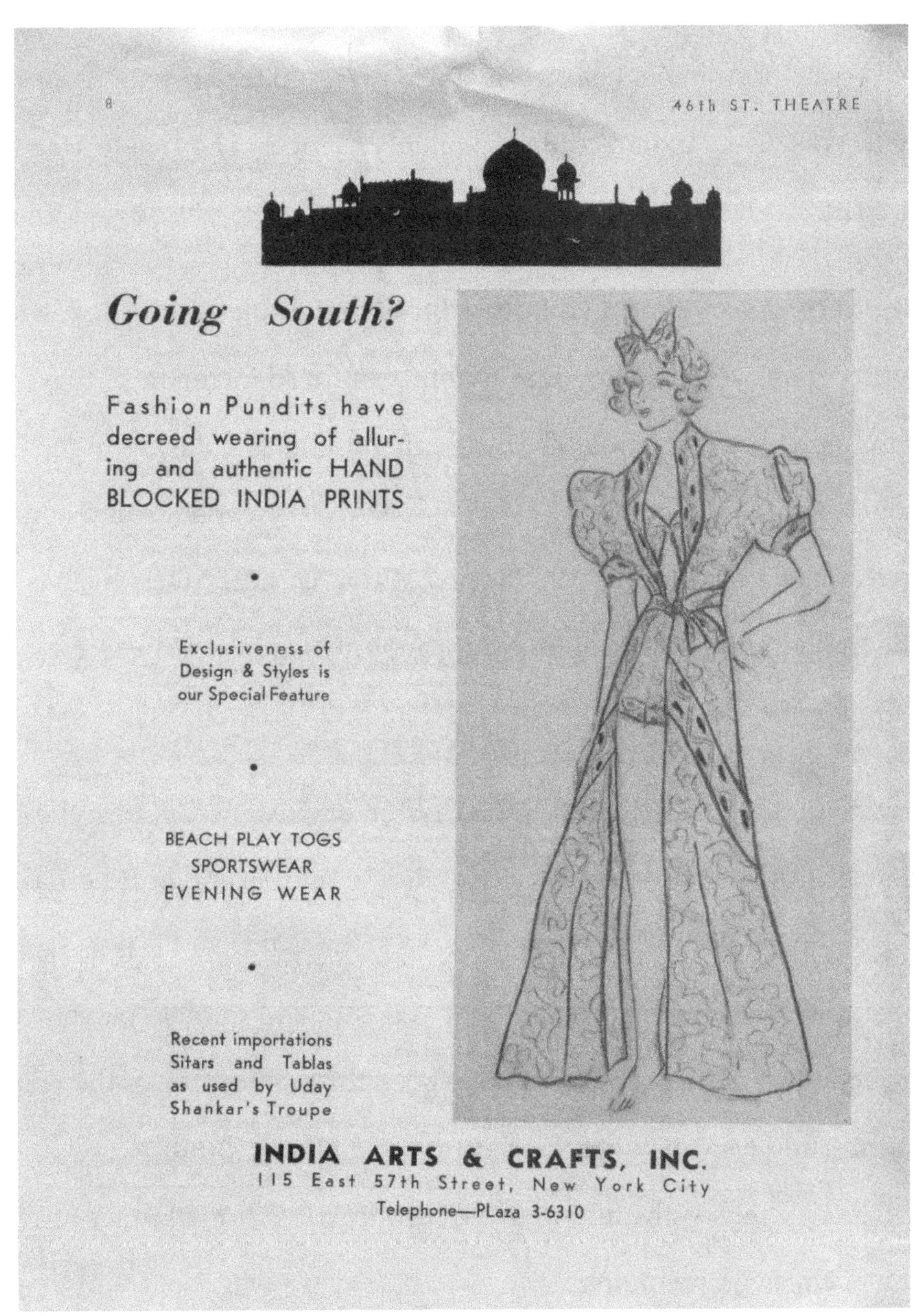

8 46th ST. THEATRE

Going South?

Fashion Pundits have decreed wearing of alluring and authentic HAND BLOCKED INDIA PRINTS

•

Exclusiveness of Design & Styles is our Special Feature

•

BEACH PLAY TOGS
SPORTSWEAR
EVENING WEAR

•

Recent importations Sitars and Tablas as used by Uday Shankar's Troupe

INDIA ARTS & CRAFTS, INC.
115 East 57th Street, New York City
Telephone—PLaza 3-6310

Kaiser Family Papers, Papers of Charles and Ray Eames at the Library of Congress, Part I, Box 283, Folder 3

An essay by Annabel Learned inside a program for another Shan-Kar performance discusses Indian culture explicitly. Titled "The Hindu Dance," Learned writes,

> The very idea of dancing has in India a special splendor. The casual writer speaks of 'dancing dust,' another of the 'dancing heat' that shimmers over the land. 'The Supreme Intelligence dances in the soul,' says the sacred book. Dawn is called a dancer adorning herself, and in the legends gods are seen dancing. From earliest times this has been to the Indian mind a natural image through which to feel the energy and wonder of creation....
>
> As the divine dance beats out the rhythm of existence, in turn the classic dance of India shows the activity of divine figures and epic heroes, or expounds an emotional theme. It is an error to think of this ancient and beautiful art as mere entertainment. Like the old miracle-players and troubadours, dancers of India have been through centuries the voice of a culture and a spirit, whether in courts of kings or countless villages. Theirs is the telling of a tradition, the vision of inner forces, and the poetic evoking of life.[116]

The final phrase, "the poetic evoking of life," is striking in its similarity to comments made about Ray and Charles Eames. Friends described their exuberance and appreciation for beauty. Ray's seemingly insatiable appetite for New York cultural events in her youth gave her an aesthetic glossary and source of inspiration for the rest of her life.

Chapter 4: Ray's Passions and Pursuits

An individual possessing voracious creative curiosity must feed it constantly. Ray pursued a variety of interests in the 1930s, effectively designing an extracurricular education that honed her talents. These pursuits included her involvement with the American Abstract Artists group, modern dance classes, photography, architecture, literature, Indian culture, interior decoration and fashion. A sculptor's fascination with structure underlay Ray's appreciation of these subjects. In the Bowman interview, she mused, "I've always been interested in structure, whatever form it was—interested in dance and music, and even my interest in literature had that base, I think—sculpture—as structure in architecture."[117]

American Abstract Artists

As one of the founding members of the American Abstract Artists group, Ray attended meetings and exhibited with other pioneering artists such as Joseph Albers, Byron Browne, Harry Holtzman, Ad Reinhardt, and David Smith. Giovannini writes:

> Most of the painters and sculptors who founded the American Abstract Artists group in 1936 were Hofmann's students. They banded together because abstract art by American artists was being ignored by the Whitney Museum of American Art, The Museum of Modern Art, and prominent galleries. The most conceptually advanced artists in New York, called America's "first truly avant-garde artists," decided to take

their own initiative, and—as they learned from the highly politicized, issue-charged decade—there was strength in union. At the studio of Piet Mondrian's leading proponent in America, Harry Holtzman, they gathered to organize a group show that would bypass the establishment that dismissed them.[118]

The 1937 General Prospectus (which Ray covered in doodles) outlines the purpose of American Abstract Artists, often abbreviated the A.A.A.:

> Our purpose is to unite American 'abstract' artists, (1) to bring before the public their individual works, (2) to foster public appreciation of this direction in painting and sculpture, (3) to afford each artist the opportunity of developing his own work by becoming familiar with the effort of others, by recognising differences as well as those elements he may have in common with them.[119]

Although Ray's friend and classmate Ben Baldwin described her work as never fully abstract, she participated in AAA exhibitions. She jokingly commented on the tension between figurative and abstract art in a 1937 letter to her mother: "have been painting on my same old still life that is practically dead now- and the darn painting gets more and more realistic by day. Looks like I'll have to follow Miss Kennedy's footsteps and resign from the A.A. A.!"[120]

Ray saved an article in the *New York Sun* published March 13, 1939. The reporter Melville Upton wrote a contemptuous review of an AAA exhibition, starting with the headline "Abstract Art Has A Showing—American Group Exhibits at Riverside Museum—Proves Decorative Display—And, Furthermore, Wins Favor in Unexpected Circles." Although Upton dislikes the exhibit, he admits, "the limousine set has taken up with abstraction in art. There were more than 700 persons present at the opening reception. The crush of cars before the museum was noticeable even on the Drive...."[121] Upton attempts to link abstraction with female foolishness:

> Fifty-three members of the fifty-eight constituting the organization are represented and between three and four hundred works are on view. In its entirety it makes a lively and highly decorative showing. *If you can escape the solicitous ministrations of young women, voluable [sic] with studio and art-appreciation-course patter, who take you kindly but firmly by the hand—figuratively speaking, of course—and insist upon guiding you through the mysteries that were fairly thoroughly explored and charted and most effectively exploited before, or at least most shortly after, these young people were born,* you may be able to spend an agreeable half hour or so wandering about the galleries and indulging in that freedom of choice that the artists themselves insist upon in expression [emphasis added].[122]

Upton seeks to undermine the American abstract movement by associating it with feminine, decorative qualities. Despite Upton's "decorative" dismissal of abstraction, the article contains words of praise for Ray's work. Her gender-ambiguous name of "Ray Kaiser" may have been an asset, for Upton includes her in his list of "artists who seem to give the exhibition its most appealing features:

> I. Rice Pereira, Werner Drewes, Hananiah Harari, Byron Browne, Ralph M. Rosenborg, Vaclav Vytlacil, R.D. Turnbull, Esphyr Slovbodkina, Louis Schanker, Charles G. Shaw, Robert J. Wolf, Harry I. Wildenberg, Paul Kelpe, Joseph Albers, Giorgio Cavallon, Susie Frelinghuysen, Fritz Glarner and *Ray Kaiser*" [emphasis added].[123]

249 ...

EXHIBITION

American Abstract Artists

O

RIVERSIDE MUSEUM, NEW YORK — March 7-26, 1939

The numbers on each exhibit correspond to the numbers below

1. Joseph Albers
2. Rosalind Bengelsdorf
3. Ilya Bolotowsky
4. Harry Bowden
5. Byron Browne
6. Jeanne Carles
7. Giorgio Cavallon
8. A. N. Christie
9. Anna Cohen
10. Burgoyne Diller
11. Werner Drewes
12. Herzl Emanuel
13. John Ferren
14. Susie Frelinghuysen
15. A. E. Gallatin
16. Fritz Glarner
17. Durnel Grant
18. Balcomb Greene
19. Gertrude Greene
20. Hananiah Harari
21. Carl R. Holty
22. Harry Holtzman
23. Dorothy Joralemon
24. Ray Kaiser
25. Gerome Kamrowski
26. Frederick Kann
27. Paul Kelpe
28. Leo Lances
29. Ibram Lassaw
30. Agnes Lyall
31. Alice Mason
32. George McNeil
33. George L. K. Morris
34. I. Rice Pereira
35. Margaret Peterson
36. A. D. F. Reinhardt
37. Ralph M. Rosenborg
38. Louis Schanker
39. Charles G. Shaw
40. Esphyr Slobodkina
41. David Smith
42. Florence Swift
43. Albert Swinden
44. R. D. Turnbull
45. Vaclav Vytlacil
46. Rudolph Weisenborn
47. Warren Wheelock
48. Frederick Whiteman
49. Harry I. Wildenberg
50. Robert J. Wolff
51. Beckford Young
52. Janet Young
53. Wilfrid Zogbaum

Ray is listed as exhibitor #24. Kaiser Family Papers, Photograph of program by the author. Papers of Charles and Ray Eames at the Library of Congress, Part I, Box 283, Folder 1

Although abstraction became much more common and accepted in the next few decades, it was still controversial in the time that Ray was exhibiting. The regionalist paintings of Thomas Hart Benton, John Steuart Curry and Grant Wood were wildly popular. American art was characterized by figurative representations of "Americanness." The lack of a definitive subject in abstract art disturbed advocates of figurative art. A questionnaire Ray saved from an abstract exhibition highlights many of the issues facing the abstract art movement, including:

> Do you believe Abstract Painting and Sculpture to be among the natural and logical expressions of a civilization such as ours today? Do you find that an Abstract Tradition, to be expressive of America today, must cut itself off completely from the lands where it originated? Or do you feel that an international style may be impending, to which the artist may bring his national, racial, and personally expressive talents? Do you believe the contemporary works by Abstract Artists to be merely a stepping-stone to a future art which is figurative? Or the start of a strong tradition in its own terms? Or a blind alley which will have to be abandoned? Do you feel that to be "alive" a work of art must draw vitality from the simulation of life in its subject matter? Or, do you feel it possible to create a living and expressive organism through combinations of form and color and line without representing definite objects?[124]

Ray's involvement with the American Abstract Artists placed her at the forefront of the movement that would shape American art for the rest of the century. She continued to be involved with the organization for many years, exhibiting work in the 1952 group show and sending in her dues to fellow member Ida Fischer who wrote back addressing her as "Buddha," Hans Hofmann's old nickname for her.[125] Abstraction eventually dominated figurative art, but Ray embraced it when it was still unpopular. Abstract forms characterize the distinctive aesthetic of Eames Office products. Ray identified the abstract quality of the 1948 Eames House in the Bowman interview: "I think the abstractness of it is appreciated and felt to be personal, eventually—the possibility of its being personal."[126]

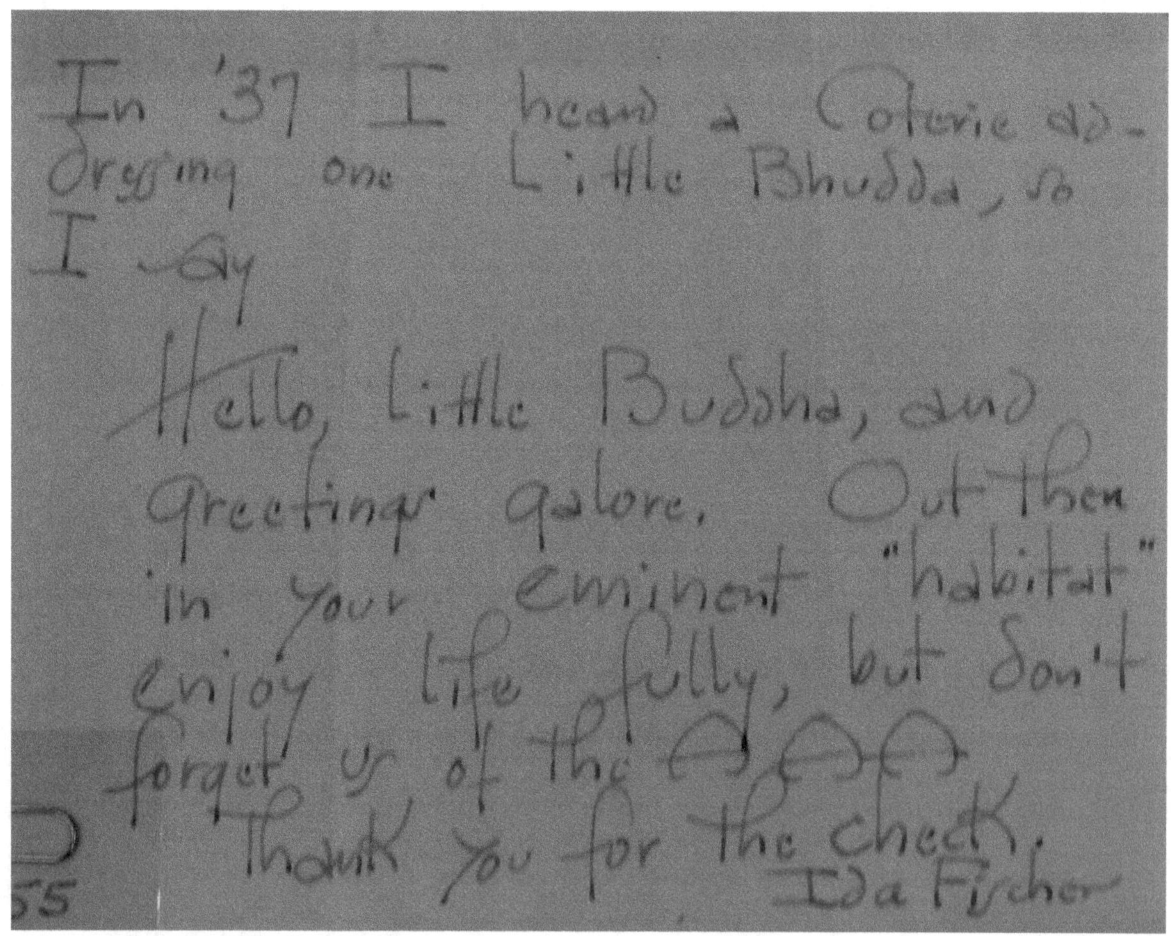

In '37 I heard a Coterie addressing one Little Bhudda, so
I say
Hello, Little Buddha, and
greetings galore. Out there
in your eminent "habitat"
enjoy life fully, but don't
forget us of the AAA
Thank you for the check.
Ida Fischer

Letter from Ida Fischer to Ray Kaiser Eames about her annual membership dues to the American Abstract Artists. Photograph of letter by the author. Papers of Charles and Ray Eames at the Library of Congress Part II, Box 1, Folder 11

Modern Dance Classes

As discussed earlier in the context of Ray's attendance of dance performances, dance was a very important part of Ray's life. She started studying dance as a child in California and trained with Carmen Rooker at the Bennett School. She continued this interest in New York, attending dance recitals and taking classes in modern dance. A letter written shortly before Ray's graduation from the Bennett School indicates Rooker advised her about opportunities to continue dancing in New York: "Miss Rooker gave me some information about the Humphrey Weidman dancers too—but I'll tell you all about it—I really am looking forward to these next years—are you?"[127] Ray discussed the variety of dancers she trained with in New York in her 1980 interview with Ruth Bowoman, and the Kaiser Family Papers contain advertisements for Hanya Holm classes saved by Ray. An October 1933 letter states Ray's intention to "start going once a week to [Mary] Wigman's school and then try to get in the Dancer's Club too."[129]

Photography

Although Ray didn't own a camera herself, she purchased one for her mother in 1933.[130] From the tone of her letters, it seems she hoped to start her mother on a photography hobby. She discussed her mother's photos and encouraged her use of the camera with comments such as "Don't forget to bring up your camera Sunday," written shortly before her graduation from Bennett School.[131] It is unclear whether Ray also used her mother's camera. Although Charles Eames was known as the principal photographer in the Eames Office, a shot from the filming of *The Powers of Ten* shows Ray concentrating behind the viewfinder of a camera.

Architecture

Charles Eames is widely credited for bringing architectural knowledge to the Eames Office, while Ray's rich background warrants only an admission of her "decorative skills" by many design scholars.[132] Two newspaper clippings in the Kaiser Family Papers indicate that Ray was interested in architecture long before meeting Charles Eames. One clipping is a photo of a severely modern house, with the caption, "Brownstone Loses Out: Right—The home of William Lescaze, architect, on East Forty-eighth Street, first example of residential modern architecture in the city."[133] The other clipping covers the reaction of Frank Lloyd Wright to the restoration of Colonial Williamsburg. Rockefeller's project "was deplored… in an espousal of 'organic' architecture" where "the dean of American architects told an audience at William and Mary College that the restoration's chief value was to 'show us how little we need this type of architecture now.'"[134] The lengthy article also includes Wright's discussion of the aims of organic architecture, and the reasons for his dislike of colonial-era buildings.[135]

Literature

Ray's appreciation of literature must be discussed in the context of her education, the nature of which has often been downplayed in her biographical sketches. Bennett School was popularly known as "a finishing school for young ladies," although it actually wasn't one while Ray studied there.[136] Kirkham includes a footnote in her book explaining that her own use of the phrase "finishing school" is based on interviews where Marilyn Neuhart and Deborah Sussman each made the point about the "finishing school," and both thought that Charles considered Ray to have a lot of "class."[137] The linkage of "finishing school" to "class" reinforces traditional female roles and obscures the fact that Ray received solid academic training at the Bennett School, not simply lessons in how to be a tasteful housewife. Bennett School was a two-year college when she attended it. In the Bowman interview, Ray explains, "an old friend who'd been to a school in the East suggested that it would be a good place to study, because it had been a wonderful experience for her. So I went to this funny school in upper New York, which was marvelous.... It had been a school that went up to college, and then later became a junior college. So I only had two years of college."[138] Charles Eames himself had only three years of college at Washington University. He studied architecture there from 1925 to 1928, when he was asked to leave "because of his general non-conformity, his 'premature enthusiasm for Frank Lloyd Wright'... and the time he spent working for one of St. Louis's busiest architectural firms, Trueblood and Graf."[139]

School papers indicate Ray received a quality education at Bennett School, including encouragement of her love of literature. Her perpetually idiosyncratic spelling (it is reproduced as is in the excerpts from her letters within this book) belies a keen interest in literature, particularly challenging authors like James Joyce. Writing her mother from Hofmann's summer session, Ray discusses her current reading:

> I get <u>no</u> time to read (at night I see Carles [Mercedes Carles Matter] for a very short time then go to bed to keep warm) but have been glancing

> at the Oddyssey [sic]—and am again enjoying it so much—. Also bought a New Yorker—Have you read the Thurber article "The Macbeth Murder Mystery"? [sic] It is a masterpiece I think. I do wish I had my Shakespeare book here—as the quiet makes it perfect for real reading—[140]

Nine days later Ray responded to newspaper clippings sent by her mother:

> I died at the [Thomas Hart] Benton clipping—sour-grapes—was very good to read the book reviews also—hope you are saving the Sunday ones—I do want to read the Hemingway book—I am starved for reading matter—books –but to take books out of the library costs $2.00-down $1.50 back and it is not in my budget—
>
> Have read the Oddysey [sic] and loved it. now [sic] am all set to tackle Ullyses [sic] (Joyce again—).[141]

References to the work of James Joyce abound in the files. Ray loved his writing. A saved *New Yorker* review of Joyce's Finnegans Wake declares, "Don't Shoot the Book-Reviewer; He's Doing The Best He Can" and

> The world would doubtless be amazed at Mr. Joyce's achievement, assuming the world understood it. But one doubts that "Finnegans Wake" will be grasped—at least in our time—except by a few conscientious philologists and a small lunatic fringe of autohypnotic Joyceans who seem able to hurl themselves into a trance of intuitive comprehension.[142]

In the Bowman interview Ray identified structure as an underlying factor for her interest in literature, and this fascination with structure seems particularly appropriate for reading Joyce. Indeed, as Eugene Jolas, a commentator quoted in the *New Yorker* review states, Joyce wants to "hammer out a verbal vision that destroys time and space."[143] The parallels between Joyce's approach to literature and the artistic concepts Ray was practicing with Hofmann are striking.

Indian Culture

India became the subject of several Eames Office Projects. Architect Donald Albrecht writes, "Alexander Girard's exhibition Textiles and Ornamental Arts of India, presented at The Museum of Modern Art in 1955, inspired their fascination with the country."[144] Ray was interested in India long before 1955, as seen in her enthusiastic following of Uday Shan-Kar's Hindu Ballet. The Eames Office helped mount Girard's exhibition and produced a film to document it. Soon afterward, the Indian government asked the Eames Office to write a report looking "for ways to prevent modern Western design and technology from overwhelming and destroying their country's traditional culture."[145] The 1958 report's purpose "was to guide India into the future and recommend how the country could industrialize and make mass-produced goods without losing the quality of its traditional handicrafts."[146] This led to months of fieldwork in India and ultimately, the establishment of a National Institute of Design.[147] In 1965 Ray returned to India for production of the Office exhibition "Nehru: His Life and His India."[148] Deborah Sussman, then a young Eames Office employee for whom Ray became something of a mentor, recalls their travels together:

> By day we explored the countryside. We were the first women to have pink turbans made and wound about our heads in the market. We had our fortunes told, fought over the same necklace as we left for Delhi. Our cameras hungrily devoured the exotic, elegant people who subsisted on next to nothing and moved like Balanchine dancers—and the

> connective tissue of their physical world, which expressed their culture in ways we could never have imagined….
>
> This time with Ray was a gift. Her capacity for adventure paralleled mine and her acute observations sharpened my own. I loved her and will be eternally fascinated by her unique sensibility and her awesome internal strength.[149]

Fashion

In a 1932 letter to her mother Ray declared she wants to earn her living "in Commercial Art—either Advertising or Costume Design."[150] This intriguing statement reveals that her career ambitions started early and identifies an interest in costume design. In January 1938 Ray wrote her mother that her friend Eleanor McClatchy "told me that 'Fran' (Francis Hayes) was to give a concert in February and wanted a costume so I drew up several designs and sent them to Eleanor—who seemed to like them very much."[151]

Many of Ray's acquaintances testify to the meticulous care with which she chose the fabric and cuts of her clothing. As an adult, Ray wore a self-fashioned uniform, noted by Eames scholars for its distinctiveness from the changing fashions of the times. Kirkham describes Ray's uniform as "simply cut blouses, jackets, and plain full skirts or pinafore dresses"[152] and theorizes,

> One source of the nostalgic, the utilitarian, and the "little girl" elements of Ray's image was Judy Garland, who wore a short pinafore dress with nipped-in waist and a soft, high-necked, short-sleeved blouse in *The Wizard of Oz*. Other films of the 1930s, the 1940s, and the early 1950s idealized late-nineteenth-century and turn-of-the-century America,

recreating a past at once pre-adult, prewar, pre-industrial, and preoccupied with women's place being in the home and subordinate to men yet offering audiences vivacious and capable young women whose independence, while contained within an acceptable femininity, was signaled by the rationality of their dress. The combination of rationality and a femininity without undue fussiness was as essential an ingredient in the style adopted by Ray Eames as it was in those favored by Hollywood's celluloid heroines.[153]

While this interpretation assumes Ray purposely highlighted "little girl" aspects of her appearance to make her active professional role in the Eames Office more acceptable, a document found in the Kaiser Family Papers suggests otherwise. The list of required clothes at the Bennett School indicates that Ray's adult fashion style was influenced not so much by feminist theory or Hollywood as simply what she wore at school. The Bennett School Uniform consisted of: "A blue woolen jumper dress / A regulation middy-blouse / A pair of Pediform black oxfords / A pair of black cotton hose."[154] This is more or less what Ray wore for the rest of her career, and Ray's choice to wear this style predates Judy Garland's wardrobe in the 1939 release of *The Wizard of Oz*. A set of private handwritten notes by Ray's friend Elaine Sewell Jones written on her personal copy of Kirkham's book takes issue with the depiction of Ray's clothing choices, describing instead that Ray had told her many times that she was locked into the silhouette that she had become associated with.[155] In this respect her adherence to an unchanging signature style and refusal to incorporate popular fashion trends can be seen as a declaration of independence from the expectations placed on women to adapt to changing fashion trends as well as a form of personal branding (much like Charles was often seen wearing a bow tie). Rather than follow fashions dictated by others, Ray remained loyal to a style that suited her.

"When and if I'm famous"

The determination of Ray's career ambitions can be seen in an eerie 1933 letter to her mother. After discussing issues regarding current items of clothing, she launches into her plan for "working clothes" completing the notes with illustrated figures modeling her ideas:

> By the way—when you get my white sweater and shirt out of the trunk will you bring up that tan number—with the lace blouse—
>
> -And don't throw away your little black velvet jacket—I just discovered I adore it—*It's also given me an idia [sic] for some "working clothes" when and if I'm famous!* Just lots of coloured skirts—and velvet jackets [emphasis added].[156]

Conclusion

Ray Eames is often viewed as Charles Eames' charming sidekick, a perky woman who was good at arranging things. In 1973, Ray and Charles' friend Esther McCoy wrote a New York Times Magazine article including Ray's involvement in the Eames Office products, but against McCoy's wishes, the publishers edited out Ray. The Library of Congress files contain a McCoy letter apologizing for the debacle. It's important to note that Charles frequently announced her involvement in the Eames Office during interviews, and that the popular identification of Eames Office designs with Charles alone was mainly an external phenomenon fueled by his charisma and talent for public appearances. Eames expert Daniel Ostroff discovered a speech Charles Eames gave to a national assembly of the American Institute of Architects (AIA) in 1952 that characterizes Charles' understanding of his working partnership with Ray:

> My wife is a painter, and a very good one, and we've been working together for, oh, twelve years now. At first I used to help and criticize things she was doing, and then she would help and criticize things I was doing, and we would pitch in and do all the jiggering for each other and get it as people do. Then, gradually, things begin to sort of entropy. Things began to get shuffled, and pretty soon you didn't know where one started and the other ended, and anything that we've looked at or talked about here, I say that I'm doing it, but actually, she's doing it just as much as I am, only she sort of goes under the same corporate type name.

> Her friends in the American Association of Abstract Artists take a very dim view of the fact that Ray hasn't exhibited any paintings or, actually, hasn't done a lot of any painting lately, in the sense that you can paint something and put it into a frame.
>
> Now, actually, I think she has been consistently functioning as a painter, and has functioned as a painter on and above the call of duty, because her hand and everything that makes it so is a part of everything we do, just as much of architecture as anything else… and if you're thinking of what some color [looks like] in relation to something else, this is not it. This is really functioning as a painter, extra and beyond perception, stuff that is anticipatory of very real things that happen later on, and it can come into the field of engineering as anything else. The contribution of an artist can often be-by his close association and feeling and contact with nature or situations, thinking again beyond the surface-to be able to have an intuitive feeling for what the appropriate form may be.[157]

The time has come to look at the history and legacy of the Eames Office anew. The output of the Eames Office is inextricably entrenched in American popular culture. As Charles himself declared, this work was not solely by Charles Eames. It was produced through collaboration with Ray.

The Library of Congress papers are a treasure trove. The researcher is sucked deeper and deeper into Ray's fascinating world. The woman in the documents is independent, vivacious, going everywhere and meeting everyone, from John Dos Pasos to Piet Mondrian. Her letters are punctuated with gutsy "Damns!" Some have characterized her as giving up painting for her husband's design career, but the pursuit of a design career incorporating the artistic principles of her training was always Ray's own dream. Even at the early date of 1938, she was excited about a friend's news of a "San Francisco show… of work in new materials for actual and specified use. I would love to try to do something for it—perhaps a Calderesque Mobile or a wall decoration or something."[159] This simply is not the child-like, insecure woman disparagingly portrayed in some previous scholarship and in our popular culture.

Ray's contributions and collaboration with Charles Eames and staff in the Eames Office are historically significant.[160] The fact that these accomplishments happened to be performed by a woman makes the history even more interesting. The Eames Office had a profound influence on the way Americans furnished and used their homes. From the affordable modern sculpture of Eames furniture to the revolutionary museum exhibitions, Ray's work shaped the aesthetic and mentality of the twentieth century.

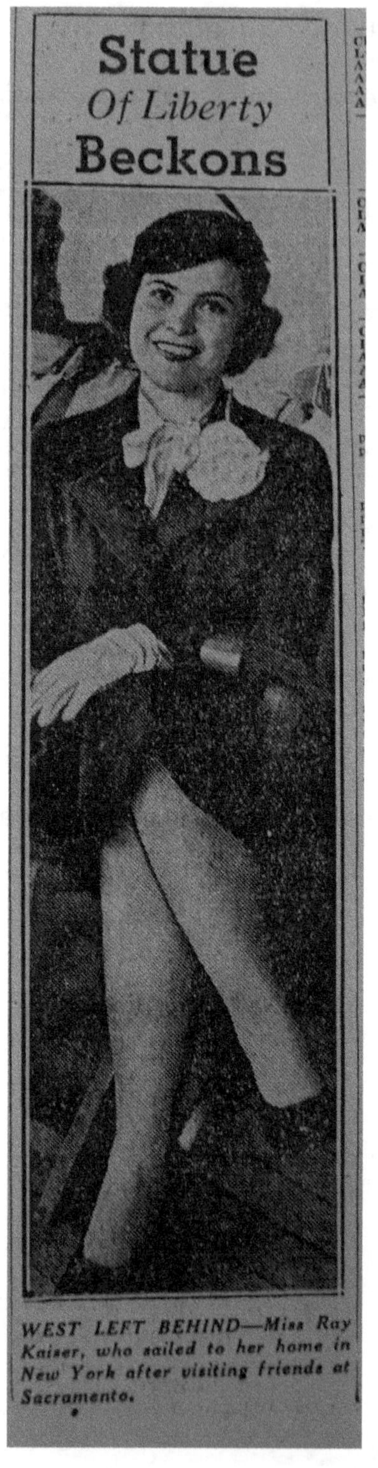

Statue
Of Liberty
Beckons

WEST LEFT BEHIND—Miss Ray Kaiser, who sailed to her home in New York after visiting friends at Sacramento.

Ray pictured in the newspaper in 1936. Kaiser Family Papers, Papers of Charles and Ray Eames at the Library of Congress, Part I, Box 278, Folder 4. Photograph of the newspaper clipping taken by the author.

Acknowledgments

I would like to express my gratitude to the many people who have assisted in my research journey and provided scholarly camaraderie, including Daniel Ostroff, Alexander and Vanessa Wendl, Genevieve Fong, Kelsey Rose Williams, Meg McAleer, Pat Kirkham, Elle Tyra, Jennifer Palmentiero, Courtney Tsahalis, Aimee Brooks, Tanzy Ward, Larissa Wild, Julie Riches, Courtney Ahlstrom Christy, and Max Avi Kaplan, and my cherished friends and colleagues who add joy to each day. The College of William & Mary gave me a research scholarship through their Monroe Scholars program that provided the initial funding for me to begin this research as an undergraduate. I am also grateful to Ray for all the inspiration she has brought me through the years, and for leaving such a delightful trail of breadcrumbs in her manuscript collection donated to the Library of Congress. Most of all, I would like to thank my mother, who never forgot her experience meeting Ray Eames while in architecture school in California, and she made sure I attended the Library of Congress Eames exhibition that started it all for me.

About the Author

Sarah Reeder is a scholar of midcentury modern design, an appraiser, and an artist. She is the founder of the firm Artifactual History Appraisal and holds Certified Membership in the Appraisers Association of America and the International Society of Appraisers. Sarah is Co-Editor of *Worthwhile Magazine* and has written and lectured about midcentury modern design for a wide variety of professional venues and publications. She is also a member of the Toad archive team, a privately curated digital archive that explores historical textiles, objects, and documents from the midcentury period. Sarah can be found online at www.artifactualhistory.com

Endnotes

---

[1] Letter, Ray Kaiser to Edna Burr Kaiser, Nov. 11, 1932, The Library of Congress, Manuscript Division, Papers of Charles and Ray Eames, Part I, Box 289, Folder 2.

[2] McAleer, Margaret H. comp. "Charles and Ray Eames: A Register of Their Papers in the Library of Congress." (http://findingaids.loc.gov/db/search/xq/searchMfer02.xq?_id=loc.mss.eadmss.ms998024&_faSection=overview&_faSubsection=scopecontent&_dmdid=d13492e23. Online. 1 Jan. 2003), pp. 10-11.

[3] The common use of Ray as a man's name led many to conclude that she was a man. The files contain several letters addressed to Mr. Ray Kaiser.

[4] "Ray" was a name associated with several members of the Kaiser family and likely carried personal significance for people like Ray's father Alexander Kaiser. I feel it is important to dispel the notion that Ray used a male name to try to gain an advantage in her career by showing the "Ray" name was part of a much older family tradition. My favorite story associated with Ray's aunt (published in the *San Francisco Call* on August 14, 1900) details how her aunt led a party of fellow visitors to a hot springs resort on an expedition to rescue and feed the starving animals of a local farmer. The farmer had been arrested as part of a feud with a relative and all the animals on his farm had gone three days without food and water and were on the brink of death. Ray's aunt is identified as a critical leader in gathering a group to feed and rescue the animals to save them from starvation.

[5] *San Francisco Call*, July 13, 1913, clipping uploaded by Ron Baublitz in 2019 and accessed in the Find A Grave database in 2021, https://www.findagrave.com/memorial/204089626/henriette-elizabeth-kaiser The spelling of "Henriette" is likely a typographical error as her grandmother was named Henrietta and the grave marker for Ray's sister in Cypress Lawn Memorial Park in Colma, California reads "Henrietta E Kaiser." Cypress Lawn Memorial Park grave information accessed 2021 at https://www.cypresslawn.com/resources/memorial-park-resources/locate-a-gravesite/

[6] "Arnold Friedberger Family: Early Jewish Pioneer Merchants in Stockton and the Gold Country of California," accessed 2021, http://www.jmaw.org/friedberger-jewish-stockton/

[7] The August, 1927 issue of *El Capitan*, the insurance company's newsletter features Kaiser's father on page 5: "One hundred consecutive months—eight and one-quarter years—of representation on the monthly Honor roll of his company, necessitating a minimum of $10,000 of new paid business each month—this is the record which Alex Kaiser, home office representative of California State Life, will soon be celebrating.

A native Californian, formerly a jeweler at Stockton but for years engaged as a theatrical manager at San Francisco and Sacramento, Mr. Kaiser joined the California State Life staff at its home office August 25, 1919."

Newspaper clipping, August 1927, The Library of Congress, Manuscript Division, Papers of Charles and Ray Eames, Part I, Box 288, Folder 3.

A newspaper clipping from the October 15, 1926 *El Capitan* gives insight into the personality of Kaiser's father: "Here's a new record of performance hung up by Alex Kaiser of Sacramento. Alex showed up at the Home Office early Monday morning of last week and engaged in conversation concerning the Appaweek Contest.

"'No man ought to have a rate book who can't turn in an app each week,' declared Kaiser. Then he went further and said anybody who really tried could write an application any day of the week. Furthermore he vouchsafed the statement that he could produce $1000 of business most any hour he went after it. So Alex checked out and was back in 25 minutes with an application. Practically the same thing occurred every day of the week..."

Newspaper clipping, Oct. 15, 1926, The Library of Congress, Manuscript Division, Papers of Charles and Ray Eames, Part I, Box 288, Folder 3.

[8] "Arnold Friedberger Family: Early Jewish Pioneer Merchants in Stockton and the Gold Country of California," accessed 2021, http://www.jmaw.org/friedberger-jewish-stockton/

[9] Eames, Ray Kaiser. Interview with Ruth Bowman. (Smithsonian Archives of American Art. http://www.aaa.si.edu/collections/interviews/oral-history-interview-ray-eames-12821#transcript 1980).

[10] The author would like to thank Daniel Ostroff, author of an Eames Anthology, for graciously sharing this information and images from his personal copy of Ray's high school yearbook.

[11] Eames, Ray Kaiser. Interview with Ruth Bowman. (Smithsonian Archives of American Art. http://www.aaa.si.edu/collections/interviews/oral-history-interview-ray-eames-12821#transcript 1980).

[12] Letter, Ray Kaiser to Edna Burr Kaiser, Jan. 16, 1933, The Library of Congress, Manuscript Division, Papers of Charles and Ray Eames, Part I, Box 289, Folder 3.

[13] Ray referred to Carles indirectly in a 1980 interview with Ruth Bowman of the Smithsonian Archives of American Art: "... I went to New York City because friends at school had heard of a wonderful painting teacher. They were ahead of me, and they had gone to study there that winter before I was out. I went then to the summer school and then went back to New York and stayed for several

years." Eames, Ray Kaiser. Interview with Ruth Bowman. (Smithsonian Archives of American Art. http://www.aaa.si.edu/oralhist/eames80.htm., 1980), p. 2; Letter, Ray Kaiser to Edna Burr Kaiser, May 15, 1933, The Library of Congress, Manuscript Division, Papers of Charles and Ray Eames, Part I, Box 289, Folder 4.

[14] Goodman, Cynthia. *Hans Hofmann.* (New York: Abbeville Press, 1986), pp. 28-29.

[15] Mercedes Carles Matter, interview with Joseph Giovannini, Aug. 25, 1996 in Joseph Giovannini, "The Office of Charles Eames and Ray Kaiser: The Material Trail," in Albrecht, Donald, Beatriz Colmina, Joseph Giovannini, Alan Lightman, Hélène Lipstadt, and Philip and Phylis Morrison. *The Work of Charles and Ray Eames: A Legacy of Invention.* (New York: Harry N. Abrams, Inc., 1997), p. 47.

[16] Letter, Ray Kaiser to Edna Burr Kaiser, Night of May 15, 1933, The Library of Congress, Manuscript Division, Papers of Charles and Ray Eames, Part I, Box 289, Folder 4.

[17] The presence of Hofmann paintings in the Eames House is documented in Kirkham, Pat. *Charles and Ray Eames: Designers of the Twentieth Century.* (Cambridge: MIT Press, 1995), p. 187; the *Time* photograph of Hans Hofmann is in Yone, James, ed. *Hans Hofmann.* (New York: Rizzoli, 2002), p. 1. The photo credit reads, "Hans Hofmann, 1951, in his Provincetown home with two Eames chairs given to him by Ray Eames and his paintings [sic], *Cataclysm: Homage to Howard Putzel*, 1945, hanging above. Photography by Maurice Beresov for *Time* Magazine."

[18] Seitz, William C. *Hans Hofmann.* (New York: The Museum of Modern Art: Doubleday & Company, Inc., 1963), p. 57.

[19] Pamphlet, 1933, The Library of Congress, Manuscript Division, Papers of Charles and Ray Eames, Part I, Box 281, Folder 5.

[20] Seitz, p. 57.

[21] Ibid., p. 57 and Wilkin, Karen. *Hans Hofmann, A Retrospective.* (New York: George Braziller, Inc., 2003), p. 133.

[22] Wilkin, p. 134.

[23] Ibid.

[24] Goodman, Cynthia. *Hans Hofmann.* (New York: Abbeville Press, 1986), p. 27; Letter, Hans Hofmann to Ray Kaiser, Dec. 31, 1933, The Library of Congress, Manuscript Division, Papers of Charles and Ray Eames, Part I, Box 280, Folder 7.

[25] Wilkin, p. 134.

[26] Bannard, Walter Darby. Hans Hofmann: A Retrospective Exhibition. (Houston: The Museum of Fine Arts, Houston, 1979), p. 9.

[29] Letter, Ray Kaiser to Edna Burr Kaiser, Oct. 4, 1933, The Library of Congress, Manuscript Division, Papers of Charles and Ray Eames, Part I, Box 289, Folder 4.

[30] Letter, Anna Clarke to Ray Kaiser, Oct. 20, 1933, The Library of Congress, Manuscript Division, Papers of Charles and Ray Eames, Part I, Box 276, Folder 11.

[31] Wilkin, p. 134.

[32] Exhibition brochure, "Lee Krasner: A Retrospective," San Francisco Museum of Modern Art, 9 February—1 April 1984, The Library of Congress, Manuscript Division, Papers of Charles and Ray Eames, Part I, Box 62, Folder 4.

[33] Pamphlet, 1935, The Library of Congress, Manuscript Division, Papers of Charles and Ray Eames, Part I, Box 281, Folder 5.

[34] Pamphlet, 1935, The Library of Congress, Manuscript Division, Papers of Charles and Ray Eames, Part I, Box 281, Folder 5.

[35] Eames Office Video Oral History Project with Eames Demetrios, Mar. 19, 1992, Sarasota, Fla., © 1997, Lucia Eames dba Eames Office., cited in Joseph Giovannini, "The Office of Charles Eames and Ray Kaiser: The Material Trail," in Albrecht, Donald, Beatriz Colmina, Joseph Giovannini, Alan Lightman, Hélène Lipstadt, and Philip and Phylis Morrison. The Work of Charles and Ray Eames: A Legacy of Invention. (New York: Harry N. Abrams, Inc., 1997), p. 56.

[36] Munro, Eleanor. Originals: American Women Artists. (New York: Simon & Schuster, Inc., 1982), p. 111.

[37] Eames, Ray Kaiser. Interview with Ruth Bowman. (Smithsonian Archives of American Art. http://www.aaa.si.edu/oralhist/eames80.htm., 1980), pp. 2-3.

[38] Ostroff, Daniel. "Ray Eames." Eames Office, available http://www.eamesoffice.com/scholars-walk/ray-eames-by-daniel-ostroff/

[39] The Library of Congress, Manuscript Division, Papers of Charles and Ray Eames, Part I, Box 281, Folder 5.

[40] In response to Ruth Bowman's question, "Whatever happened to all your paintings that you did when you worked with Hofmann?" Ray answered, "Most of them are lost. I had some in storage, and I didn't do that much painting all those years. I drew a great deal and I have some. But many of them were lost in

storage." Ibid., p. 33.

[41] Eames Office Video Oral History Project with Eames Demetrios, Mar. 19, 1992, Sarasota, Fla., © 1997, Lucia Eames dba Eames Office., cited in Joseph Giovannini, "The Office of Charles Eames and Ray Kaiser: The Material Trail," in Albrecht, Donald, Beatriz Colmina, Joseph Giovannini, Alan Lightman, Hélène Lipstadt, and Philip and Phylis Morrison. *The Work of Charles and Ray Eames: A Legacy of Invention*. (New York: Harry N. Abrams, Inc., 1997), pp. 56-57.

[42] Mercedes Carles Matter, interview with Joseph Giovannini, Aug. 25, 1996, cited in Joseph Giovannini, "The Office of Charles Eames and Ray Kaiser: The Material Trail," in Albrecht, Donald, Beatriz Colmina, Joseph Giovannini, Alan Lightman, Hélène Lipstadt, and Philip and Phylis Morrison. *The Work of Charles and Ray Eames: A Legacy of Invention*. (New York: Harry N. Abrams, Inc., 1997), p. 57.

[43] Eames, Ray Kaiser. Interview with Ruth Bowman. (Smithsonian Archives of American Art. http://www.aaa.si.edu/oralhist/eames80.htm., 1980), p. 34.

[44] Ibid., p. 34.

[45] Hofmann, Hans. Sara T. Weeks and Bartlett H. Hayes, Jr., eds. *Search for the Real and Other Essays*. (Cambridge: The M.I.T. Press, 1967), p. 40.

[46] Ibid., p. 44.

[47] Notes, "Notes on Hofmann's Lectures by Ray Kaiser," 1933, The Library of Congress, Manuscript Division, Papers of Charles and Ray Eames, Box 281, Folder 6. Ray spelled her nickname "Buddha," with two "d"s. Hofmann's New Year's Card addressed to "Budha" was misspelled, which is likely influenced by his relatively new acquaintance with communicating in English.

[48] Notes, "Notes on Hofmann's Lectures by Ray Kaiser," 1933, The Library of Congress, Manuscript Division, Papers of Charles and Ray Eames, Box 281, Folder 6.

[49] Eames, Ray Kaiser. Interview with Ruth Bowman. (Smithsonian Archives of American Art. http://www.aaa.si.edu/oralhist/eames80.htm., 1980), p. 2.

[50] Goodman, Cynthia. *Hans Hofmann*. (New York: Abbeville Press, 1986), p. 8.

[51] Hofmann, Hans. *Hans Hofmann: The Years 1947-1952*. Essay by Irving Sandler. (New York: André Emmerich Gallery, 1976), pp. 1-2.

[52] Ibid., p. 1.

[53] Wilkin, p. 134.

[54] The Estate of Hans Hofmann, http://www.hanshofmann.org/bio.htm, accessed 2005.

[55] Hofmann, Hans. Sara T. Weeks and Bartlett H. Hayes, Jr., eds. Search for the Real and Other Essays. (Cambridge: The M.I.T. Press, 1967), p. 45.

[56] Receipt, "Railway Express Agency—Uniform Express Receipt," Ray Kaiser to Hans Hofmann, Dec. 19, 1938, The Library of Congress, Manuscript Division, Papers of Charles and Ray Eames, Part I, Box 281, Folder 5.

[57] Eames, Ray Kaiser. Interview with Ruth Bowman. (Smithsonian Archives of American Art. http://www.aaa.si.edu/oralhist/eames80.htm., 1980), p. 2.

[58] Pamphlet, The Library of Congress, Manuscript Division, Papers of Charles and Ray Eames, Box 281, Folder 5.

[60] Programs, 1929-1939, The Library of Congress, Manuscript Division, The Papers of Charles and Ray Eames, Part I, Box 282, Folder 7-Box 283, Folder 2, Box 285, Folder 1-Box 287, Folder 7, Box 284, Folder 1-Box 284, Folder 6, Box 283, Folder 3-Box 283, Folder 4, Box 283, Folder 5.
An idea of the scale of Ray's attendance of New York cultural events can be gleaned from the size of her program collection. The inventory of all programs and selected newspaper clippings in the Kaiser Family Papers prepared in the research for my original honor's thesis numbered 109 typed pages.

[61] Joseph Giovannini, "The Office of Charles Eames and Ray Kaiser: The Material Trail," in Albrecht, Donald, Beatriz Colmina, Joseph Giovannini, Alan Lightman, Hélène Lipstadt, and Philip and Phylis Morrison. *The Work of Charles and Ray Eames: A Legacy of Invention.* (New York: Harry N. Abrams, Inc., 1997), pp. 45-46.

[62] Programs, 1929-1939, The Library of Congress, Manuscript Division, Papers of Charles and Ray Eames, Part I, Box 282, Folder 8.

[63] Billy Wilder/Kirkham, 1993 in Kirkham, Pat. *Charles and Ray Eames: Designers of the Twentieth Century.* (Cambridge: MIT Press, 1995), p. 188.

[64] Kirkham, Pat. *Charles and Ray Eames: Designers of the Twentieth Century.* (Cambridge: MIT Press, 1995), pp. 250-252.

[65] Constable, Anne. "Former Director of Folk-Art Museum dies at 84." *Santa Fe New Mexican* (2 Jul. 2003), B4.

[66] Magazine clippings, The Library of Congress, Manuscript Division, Papers of Charles and Ray Eames, Part I, Box 32, Folders 7 and 9.

[67] Cynthia Goodman cites Léger paintings were one of the few possessions Miz Hofmann took with her when she left Germany: "some of her husband's work; paintings by Georges Braque, Fernand Léger, Joan Miró, Louis Marcoussis; some pieces of Biedermeier furniture; and her extensive collection of canvases by the French primitive master Louis Vivin."

Lillian Kiesler and Fritz Bultman, interview with Cynthia Goodman, New York, March 10, 1978, cited in Goodman, Cynthia. *Hans Hofmann.* (New York: Abbeville Press, 1986), p. 31.

[69] Programs, The Library of Congress, Manuscript Division, Papers of Charles and Ray Eames, Part I, Box 282, Folder 7, Box 283, Folders 1 and 2.

[70] Program, The Library of Congress, Manuscript Division, Papers of Charles and Ray Eames, Part I, Box 283, Folder 2.

[71] Two undated newspaper clippings are titled "Surrealistic Art Called FoulPlot [sic] of Communists: Defenders of Democracy Get Madder and Madder Over That Fur-Lined Cup" and "Man Ray Finds Surrealist's Art Like New Deal: Ultra-Modern Painters and President Misunderstood by Opponents, He States."

Newspaper Clippings, The Library of Congress, Manuscript Division, Papers of Charles and Ray Eames, Part I, Box 278, Folder 6.

[72] Advertisement, The Library of Congress, Manuscript Division, Papers of Charles and Ray Eames, Part I, Box 278, Folder 6.

[73] Letter, Ray Kaiser to Edna Burr Kaiser, April 3, 1939, The Library of Congress, Manuscript Division, Papers of Charles and Ray Eames, Part I, Box 289, Folder 4.

[74] Newspaper Clipping, Mar. 12, 1939, *The New York Times Magazine*, The Library of Congress, Manuscript Division, Papers of Charles and Ray Eames, Part I, Box 278, Folder 5.

[78] Photograph and notes, The Library of Congress, Manuscript Division, Papers of Charles and Ray Eames, Part I, Box 117, Folder 7.

[79] See Pat Kirkham, "Ch. 4: Functioning Decoration" in *Charles and Ray Eames: Designers of the Twentieth Century.* (Cambridge: MIT Press, 1995), pp. 143-199 and Joseph Giovannini's essay "The Office of Charles Eames and Ray Kaiser: The Material Trail" in Albrecht et al., *The Work of Charles and Ray Eames: A Legacy of Invention.* (New York: Harry N. Abrams, Inc., 1997), pp. 45-71.

[80] Newspaper clipping, *The Sacramento Bee*, 1917, The Library of Congress, Manuscript Division, Papers of Charles and Ray Eames, Part I, Box 288, Folder 4.

In response to a question in one of her mother's letters, Ray answered, "I don't remember Daddy speaking of that vaudeville team."

Letter, Ray Kaiser to Edna Burr Kaiser, The Library of Congress, Manuscript Division, Papers of Charles and Ray Eames, Part I, Box 289, Folder 4.

[81] Letter, Ray Kaiser to Edna Burr Kaiser, Mar. 7, 1933, The Library of Congress, Manuscript Division, Papers of Charles and Ray Eames, Part I, Box 289, Folder 4.

[82] Program, The Library of Congress, Manuscript Division, Papers of Charles and Ray Eames, Part I, Box 287, Folder 3.

[83] Program, The Library of Congress, Manuscript Division, Papers of Charles and Ray Eames, Part I, Box 285, Folder 5.

[84] Program, The Library of Congress, Manuscript Division, Papers of Charles and Ray Eames, Part I, Box 285, Folder 2.

[85] Letter, Ray Kaiser to Edna Burr Kaiser, Jan. 31, 1938, The Library of Congress, Manuscript Division, Papers of Charles and Ray Eames, Part I, Box 289, Folder 9.

[86] Program, The Library of Congress, Manuscript Division, Papers of Charles and Ray Eames, Part I, Box 283, Folder 5.

[87] Program, The Library of Congress, Manuscript Division, Papers of Charles and Ray Eames, Part I, Box 283, Folder 5.

[88] Program, May 9, 1936, The Library of Congress, Manuscript Division, Papers of Charles and Ray Eames, Part I, Box 283, Folder 5.

---

[89] Eames, Ray Kaiser. Interview with Ruth Bowman. (Smithsonian Archives of American Art. http://www.aaa.si.edu/oralhist/eames80.htm., 1980), p. 34.

[90] Program, "Sonata Recital. Jo Hawthorne, Violin, Richard Malaby, Piano. Provincetown Art Association. Sunday Evening, July 28th At 8:45," July, 28, n.d., The Library of Congress, Manuscript Division, Papers of Charles and Ray Eames, Part I, Box 284, Folder 6.

[92] Eames, Ray Kaiser. Interview with Ruth Bowman. (Smithsonian Archives of American Art. http://www.aaa.si.edu/oralhist/eames80.htm. 1980), p. 27.

[93] Ray's friendship with Armenian refugee Arshile Gorky raises the questions about why she attended this particular opera. Perhaps Ray simply wanted to hear "La Traviata," or maybe her association with Gorky had an impact on how she felt about the fundraiser's beneficiary. In 1938 she went with Gorky to the Newark Air Port to view his murals. After describing their appearance to her mother, she added. "But Gorki [sic] is still Gorki—for in the map he added a second Florida on the other side of the Gulf of Mexico to make the form more pleasing—."

Letter, Ray Kaiser to Edna Burr Kaiser, Mar. 29, 1938, The Library of Congress, Manuscript Division, Papers of Charles and Ray Eames, Part I, Box 289, Folder 9.

[94] Program, The Library of Congress, Manuscript Division, Papers of Charles and Ray Eames, Part I, Box 284, Folder 2.

[95] Program, Mar. 21, 1934, The Library of Congress, Manuscript Division, Papers of Charles and Ray Eames, Part I, Box 284, Folder 2.

[96] *Blacktop: A Story of the Washing of a School Play Yard* used Bach's Goldberg Variations as the soundtrack. Kirkham, Pat. *Charles and Ray Eames: Designers of the Twentieth Century.* (Cambridge: MIT Press, 1995), p. 337.

[97] Eames/Kirkham, 1983 in Kirkham, Pat. *Charles and Ray Eames: Designers of the Twentieth Century.* (Cambridge: MIT Press, 1995), p. 329.

[98] Programs, The Library of Congress, Manuscript Division, Papers of Charles and Ray Eames, Part I, Box 284, Folders 1, 6.

[99] Program, The Library of Congress, Manuscript Division, Papers of Charles and Ray Eames, Part I, Box 284, Folder 2.

[100] Program, The Library of Congress, Manuscript Division, Papers of Charles and Ray Eames, Part I, Box 284, Folder 6.

[101] Ray discusses her dance training in detail in her 1980 interview with Ruth Bowman which I have included below for context:

"RUTH BOWMAN: One of the things that I did want to do, before we close this taping, is to talk a little bit about things that I know about that we forgot to talk about, and one of them was that you made a reference to your interest in the dance.

RAY KAISER EAMES: Yes, that goes back for a long, long time. As a child I studied -- oh, I'm so fortunate -- I naturally feel they're very closely related -- movement and -- it sounds stupid, everyone thinks so, I'm sure. But my introduction was early, it was a very, very good teacher. Did we not talk about it?

RUTH BOWMAN: No.

RAY KAISER EAMES: Leila Maple. Oh, this marvelous woman had been a member of the Russian Ballet, long, long, long ago, so her training was pure, and she turned it over to the children in the same pure state.

RUTH BOWMAN: In California?

RAY KAISER EAMES: In California, in Sacramento. A marvelous woman, who was beautiful and strong and gentle and strict -- all the great things in a teacher, you know, and so I felt that was a most fortunate happening. Then, at school, -- oh, at that time also, again, I felt fortunate that doctors at that time said children should not be on their toes, so that was eliminated, you know. Naturally, my parents had been interested in ballet. I know when Pavlova came to the West Coast they had arranged for -- I wasn't there, but my brother was there as a baby and my mother watched from the wings -- she would come out and kiss my brother and she would come back, and my mother said that she realized afterwards that she would take off her slippers and throw them away after each performance. Her toe slippers were soft -- I hadn't known that -- and there were little holes at the end, at the bottom of each one, and there they were, you know -- not thought about, you know, saving them. Anyway, I was terribly fortunate at a very early age to have seen one performance of the great Pavlova. But anyway, after that, because a teacher in school had been a student of Doris Humphrey, and had studied briefly with Mary Wigman in Germany -- did you ever see her?

RUTH BOWMAN: No, although I saw Doris Humphrey.

RAY KAISER EAMES: Oh, Wigman was so extraordinary as a dancer, just extraordinary! So it was wonderful to have that experience, because also at the school they gave yearly performances of Greek drama, using dance.

RUTH BOWMAN: This was a college?

RAY KAISER EAMES: It was a school -- it later became a junior college, but it wasn't called that then. It was called Bennett School.

RUTH BOWMAN: And Doris Humphrey was on the faculty?

RAY KAISER EAMES: No, a student of Doris Humphrey's. Her name was Carmen Rooker, but she knew all these people. The people at school were interested in -- well, in all sorts of things -- music and drama and dance, among other things. They had people visiting all the time. Mary Wigman would come and visit and loved the stage they had built, which had a wonderful resounding floor, so that was -- it had to be that close to something. And later on, after that, I went to -- I studied briefly with Hanya Holme who was a disciple/student and later representative of Wigman. And then also because of these two things I was interested in [Martha] Graham -- I think the combination of the two things -- I knew there was a link someplace -- like the overlapping lines of that diagram. Graham had certain restrictions, and Hanya Holme had, and I knew there was something in between, so I was very interested and worked with Graham. I never thought of actually performing -- I was studying to gain knowledge of movement and body and space, which is related to painting, which is related to Hofmann which is related to music and architecture, actually. Which I feel was a preparation, in my way, for later work in terms of architectural design. They all seemed interwoven. You asked me about the person who told me about Cranbrook. But also, I think the underlying element, early on, was Leila Maple. Besides the influence of my parents, and of teachers at school that had been impressive at an early age, was the sense of discipline and devotion -- being able to accomplish something. Because certainly she had it, certainly everyone I've thought of that -- Hofmann certainly had it -- Graham certainly had it, Hanya Holme, Wigman, and all the people at school had it as well." Eames, Ray Kaiser. Interview with Ruth Bowman. (Smithsonian Archives of American Art. http://www.aaa.si.edu/oralhist/eames80.htm 1980)

102 Programs, The Library of Congress, Manuscript Division, Papers of Charles and Ray Eames, Part I, Box 283, Folders 3 and 4.

103 Program, The Library of Congress, Manuscript Division, Papers of Charles and Ray Eames, Part I, Box, 283, Folder 4.

104 Program, The Library of Congress, Manuscript Division, Papers of Charles and Ray Eames, Part I, Box 283, Folder 4.

[105] Program, The Library of Congress, Manuscript Division, Papers of Charles and Ray Eames, Part I, Box 283, Folder 3.

[106] Program, The Library of Congress, Manuscript Division, Papers of Charles and Ray Eames, Part I, Box 283, Folder 3.

[107] Letter, Ray Kaiser to Edna Burr Kaiser, March 22, 1938, The Library of Congress, Manuscript Division, Papers of Charles and Ray Eames, Part I, Box 289, Folder 9.

[108] Letter, Ray Kaiser to Edna Burr Kaiser, October 4, 1933, The Library of Congress, Manuscript Division, Papers of Charles and Ray Eames, Part I, Box 289, Folder 4.

Ray took a number of dance classes in the 1930s.

[113] Program, Mar. 1, 1936, The Library of Congress, Manuscript Division, Papers of Charles and Ray Eames, Part I, Box 283, Folder 4.

[114] Program, Nov. 24, 1935, The Library of Congress, Manuscript Division, Papers of Charles and Ray Eames, Part I, Box 284, Folder 1.

[115] Program, Feb. 22, n.d., The Library of Congress, Manuscript Division, Papers of Charles and Ray Eames, Part I, Box 283, Folder 3.

[116] Program, "The Hindu Dance" by Annabel Learned, The Library of Congress, Manuscript Division, Papers of Charles and Ray Eames, Part I, Box 283, Folder 3.

[117] Eames, Ray Kaiser. Interview with Ruth Bowman. (Smithsonian Archives of American Art. http://www.aaa.si.edu/oralhist/eames80.htm 1980), p. 3.

[118] Larsen, Susan C., "The American Abstract Artists Group: A History and Evaluation of Its Impact upon American Art" (Ph.D. Diss., Evanston, Ill., Northwestern University, 1975; reprinted in Ann Arbor, Michigan, University Microfilms International), cited in Joseph Giovannini, "The Office of Charles Eames and Ray Kaiser: The Material Trail," in Albrecht, Donald, Beatriz Colmina, Joseph Giovannini, Alan Lightman, Hélène Lipstadt, and Philip and Phylis Morrison. The Work of Charles and Ray Eames: A Legacy of Invention. (New York: Harry N. Abrams, Inc., 1997), p. 58.

[119] General Prospectus, American Abstract Artists, 1937, The Library of Congress, Manuscript Division, Papers of Charles and Ray Eames, Part I, Box 276, Folder 10.

[120] Letter, Ray Kaiser to Edna Burr Kaiser, Oct. 17, 1937, The Library of Congress, Manuscript Division, Papers of Charles and Ray Eames, Part I, Box 289, Folder 8. Ray seems to be referring to the artist Marie Kennedy, identified along with Ray as a founding member of the American Abstract Artists on the group's official website at http://www.americanabstractartists.org/members.htm.

[121] Newspaper clipping, *The New York Sun*, March 13, 1939, The Library of Congress, Manuscript Division, Papers of Charles and Ray Eames, Part I, Box 276, Folder 10.

[122] Newspaper clipping, *The New York Sun*, March 13, 1939, The Library of Congress, Manuscript Division, Papers of Charles and Ray Eames, Part I, Box 276, Folder 10.

[123] Newspaper clipping, *The New York Sun*, March 13, 1939, The Library of Congress, Manuscript Division, Papers of Charles and Ray Eames, Part I, Box 276, Folder 10.

[124] Survey, The Library of Congress, Manuscript Division, Papers of Charles and Ray Eames, Part I, Box 276, Folder 10.

[125] The Library of Congress, Manuscripts Division, Papers of Charles and Ray Eames, Part II, Box 1, Folder 11.

[126] Eames, Ray Kaiser. Interview with Ruth Bowman. (Smithsonian Archives of American Art. http://www.aaa.si.edu/oralhist/eames80.htm. 1980), p. 7.

[127] Letter, Ray Kaiser to Edna Burr Kaiser, May 18, 1933, The Library of Congress, Manuscript Division, Papers of Charles and Ray Eames, Part I, Box 289, Folder 4.

[129] Letter, Ray Kaiser to Edna Burr Kaiser, Oct. 6, 1933, The Library of Congress, Manuscript Division, Papers of Charles and Ray Eames, Part I, Box 289, Folder 4.

[130] The Library of Congress, Manuscript Division, Papers of Charles and Ray Eames, Box 289, Folder 4.

[131] Letter, Ray Kaiser to Edna Burr Kaiser, May 15, 1933, The Library of Congress, Manuscript Division, Papers of Charles and Ray Eames, Part I, Box 289, Folder 4.

[132] Kirkham writes, "One problem involved in assessing Ray's role in the Eames partnership is that, besides a strong feel for structure, her strengths included an extraordinary sense of color and form and a remarkable ability to arrange groups of objects and 'decorate' interiors, be they domestic or exhibition spaces. There is no doubt that these talents contributed significantly to the products that emerged from the Eames Office, as did Ray's sense of structure, but their designation as concerned with decoration and 'prettiness' meant that they were viewed (partly

correctly) as part of women's traditional concerns with beautifying and decorating the home and consequently marginalized by those who saw them as less important than structure and technology. Paradoxically, those who could not accept that Ray might play a significant role in the 'male' spheres of architecture and furniture design acknowledged, albeit patronizingly, her abilities as a 'decorator' and her brilliance with color because these supposedly less 'important' areas were ones in which it was deemed acceptable and respectable for women's design talents to flourish." Kirkham footnotes 'Shock-proof furniture," *Architectural Forum*, April 1946, p. 10; Doris Saatchi, 'All about Eames,' *House and Garden*, February 1984, p. 129.
Kirkham, Pat. Charles and Ray Eames: Designers of the Twentieth Century. (Cambridge: MIT Press, 1995), p. 85.

[133] Newspaper clipping, The Library of Congress, Manuscript Division, Papers of Charles and Ray Eames, Part I, Box 278, Folder 5.

[134] Newspaper clipping, The Library of Congress, Manuscript Division, Papers of Charles and Ray Eames, Part I, Box 278, Folder 5.

[135] Ironically, one of the three known buildings by Charles Eames and his 1930s partner Robert Walsh was Dinsmoor House, a colonial revival home based directly on Carter's Grove. Kirkham, Pat. Charles and Ray Eames: Designers of the Twentieth Century. (Cambridge: MIT Press, 1995), pp. 18-20.

[136] Kirkham, Pat. Charles and Ray Eames: Designers of the Twentieth Century. (Cambridge: MIT Press, 1995), p. 33.

[137] Ibid., p. 413.

[138] Eames, Ray Kaiser. Interview with Ruth Bowman. (Smithsonian Archives of American Art. http://www.aaa.si.edu/oralhist/eames80.htm. 1980), pp. 1-2.

[139] Kirkham, Pat. Charles and Ray Eames: Designers of the Twentieth Century. (Cambridge: MIT Press, 1995), p. 12.

[140] Letter, Ray Kaiser to Edna Burr Kaiser, Oct. 14, 1937, The Library of Congress, Manuscript Division, Papers of Charles and Ray Eames, Part I, Box 289, Folder 8.

[141] Letter, Ray Kaiser to Edna Burr Kaiser, Oct. 23, 1937, The Library of Congress, Part I, Box 289, Folder 8.

[142] Magazine clipping, *The New Yorker*, May 6, 1939, The Library of Congress, Manuscript Division, Papers of Charles and Ray Eames, Part I, Box 278, Folder 6.

[143] Magazine clipping, *The New Yorker*, May 6, 1939, The Library of Congress, Manuscript Division, Papers of Charles and Ray Eames, Part I, Box 278, Folder 6.

[144] Albrecht, Donald, "Design Is a Method of Action," in Albrecht, Donald, Beatriz Colmina, Joseph Giovannini, Alan Lightman, Hélène Lipstadt, and Philip and Phylis Morrison. The Work of Charles and Ray Eames: A Legacy of Invention. (New York: Harry N. Abrams, Inc., 1997), p. 33.

[145] Ibid., p. 33.

[146] Ibid., p. 33.

[147] Ibid., p. 33. Albrecht states that there were three months of fieldwork; Kirkham states five months. Kirkham, p. 281.

[148] Alexander Girard was involved in this exhibition; Kirkham, p. 287; Ray discusses the India Projects at length in her interview with Ruth Bowman. Eames, Ray Kaiser. Interview with Ruth Bowman. (Smithsonian Archives of American Art. http://www.aaa.si.edu/oralhist/eames80.htm. 1980), pp. 25-26.

[149] Ibid., pp. 184-185.

[150] Letter, Ray Kaiser to Edna Burr Kaiser, Jan. 7, 1932, The Library of Congress, Manuscript Division, Papers of Charles and Ray Eames, Part I, Box 288, Folder 14.

[151] Letter, Ray Kaiser to Edna Burr Kaiser, Jan. 31, 1938, The Library of Congress, Manuscript Division, Papers of Charles and Ray Eames, Part I, Box 289, Folder 9.

[152] Kirkham, Pat. Charles and Ray Eames: Designers of the Twentieth Century. (Cambridge: MIT Press, 1995), p. 61.

[153] Ibid., p. 67.

[154] The Library of Congress, Manuscript Division, Papers of Charles and Ray Eames, Part I, Box 277, Folder 1.

[155] The author is grateful to Daniel Ostroff for sharing his scans of these notes on her hand-written copy.

[156] Letter, Ray Kaiser to Edna Burr Kaiser, March 31, 1933, The Library of Congress, Manuscript Division, Papers of Charles and Ray Eames, Part I, Box 289, Folder 4.

[157] Ostroff, Daniel, ed. An Eames Anthology. (New Haven: Yale University Press, 2015), p. 110.

[159] Letter, Ray Kaiser to Edna Burr Kaiser, Mar. 29, 1938, The Library of Congress, Manuscript Division, Papers of Charles and Ray Eames, Part I, Box 289, Folder 9.

[160] It is worth noting that Ray did not perform the typical duties of a housewife—cooks and maids were hired to perform these chores, leaving her free to work full-time at the Office. This is discussed briefly in Kirkham, pp. 375-376.

www.ingramcontent.com/pod-product-compliance
Lightning Source LLC
LaVergne TN
LVHW081252100826
845148LV00009B/1202

* 9 7 9 8 9 8 5 5 4 2 3 0 1 *